WOMEN
IN THE
WORD

WOMEN
IN THE
WORD
Sylvia Charles

Bridge Publishing, Inc.
Publishers of:
LOGOS • HAVEN • OPEN SCROLL

All Scriptures are quoted from the King James Version of the Bible unless otherwise identified.

Women in the Word
Copyright © 1984 Bridge Publishing, Inc.
All rights reserved.
Printed in the United States of America
ISBN 0-88270-579-2
Library of Congress Catalog Card Number: 84-72958

Bridge Publishing, Inc.
South Plainfield, NJ 07080

In loving dedication to my mother,
Euseba Whitaker,
the first woman to share
the Word of God with me.

TABLE OF CONTENTS

WOMEN IN THE WORD

WOMEN IN THE WORD

INTRODUCTION

This is a series of meditations for women, based upon the lives and experiences of sixty-four women whom God has given us in His Word.

These are real women with real problems, real joys, and real sorrows from all walks of life. They lived long ago, yet they can speak to us in our modern culture because the heart of a woman has not changed through the centuries. God's Word was as true for them in their day as it is for us in ours.

Except for the chapters about the women of the four Gospels, which are arranged in a more chronological order, these meditations are listed in the order they appear in Scripture. Each meditation lifts up one teaching from the Word and is not meant to be a complete study of the life and character of the woman involved. The book, therefore, may be read from beginning to end, or chapter by chapter, according to the desire to relate to a particular subject or woman.

The stories of the women in Scripture are not complete without the final chapter and the realization that we, as the Bride of Jesus Christ, have the most honored position of all the women in the Word.

It is my prayer that these meditations on the lives of the women in the Word will so minister His Word to women today that we may be better prepared to be that holy, beautiful Bride of Christ, the only begotten Son of God.

EVE

A WOMAN WHO LET DOUBT CONTROL HER MIND

Gen. 2:18-3:20; 1 Tim. 2:13-15

> But I fear, lest by any means, as the serpent beguiled Eve through his subtilty, so your minds should be corrupted from the simplicity that is in Christ. 2 Cor. 11:3

Have you ever considered the honor to be chosen of God to be the first woman on earth, to live in the most perfect place that God could design, and to be the wife of a man who had dominion over every living thing? Incomprehensible, isn't it?

Furthermore, this woman had been uniquely made. Adam had been formed from the dust of the ground. Eve was not of the earth, nor the offspring of another human being, but of the bone and flesh of her husband; she was one of a kind. Eve was indeed somebody very special.

With all these circumstances in her favor, Eve fell into the hands of Satan by listening to just one question. She, who had everything, began to doubt God and His goodness when the devil, in disguise, asked, "Yea, hath God said?" God had very definitely said what Adam and she were not allowed to

1

do, but the seed of rebellion flowered within her heart with a series of questions which we can assume went through her mind:

"Didn't God give the commandment of not eating from the tree before I was even made?"

"Am I expected to take my husband's word for it?"

"If God wanted me to do something, why didn't He tell me directly?"

"Besides, what is wrong with having knowledge of good and evil? Perhaps we need it to help us subdue the earth!"

With rationalization and justification Eve was soon in rebellion against God. Sin entered her life as she let her mind entertain questions which led to doubt and disobedience.

John tells us that Satan is overcome by the blood of the Lamb as well as by the word of our testimony (Rev. 12:11). Our mind is the door through which doubts come to us. It is the playground for disobedient thoughts, as well as a place where we can learn to bring captive every thought into the obedience of Christ (2 Cor. 10:5). Just as the doors to the homes of the Israelites had to be sprinkled with blood so that the angel of death would pass over them, so we can ask the Lord to put the blood of Jesus over the door of our minds that no thought may enter that will deliver us into the hands of our enemy, Satan, the accuser of the brethren.

We need not only this protection of the blood of Jesus, but also the word of our testimony. This word may be the testimony of how Jesus, the Living Word, is at work in our lives, or it may be telling how God's written Word has helped us in some way.

It is His Word which renews our minds so that we can have the mind of Christ. It is that constant meditation on God's Word which will dispel all doubt. For faith is the opposite of doubt and faith comes by hearing the Word of God. Likewise, doubt comes by listening to the enemy of God.

Doubt usually begins with one little question, "Hath God said?" When Satan gets us questioning God's Word, he knows that we will soon fall into disobedience. Eve paid a great price. She, who had been uniquely made, who lived in the perfect surroundings, who had every need met, who had her husband all to herself, and who was blessed with intimate communion with God, lost all of this and was given a punishment instead. God told her that she, and all women thereafter, would have sorrow in childbirth. God then put wives under the rule of their husbands because of their vulnerability to Satan. She and Adam were banished from the Garden, and he was made to till the ground, which was cursed. God had provided so much, but, by listening to one question of Satan, who wanted her to doubt God, she lost it all!

Dear God, my Maker, I thank you for your perfect plan for my life, and your desire for me to have an abundant life. I thank you, too, that you gave me a mind and a will and a freedom to choose how I will use my mind. Help me not to listen to the Enemy as he would put all kinds of questions into my mind. Instead, I ask now that the blood of Jesus cover my thoughts so that I might stand against all doubts that would come my way through people and circumstances around me. Teach me, I pray, to meditate on your Word day and night that I might have your mind, the mind of Jesus Christ. Help me to be an overcomer in the battle for my mind. In the name of Jesus, who shed His blood for me. Amen.

SARAH

A WOMAN WHO WAS "USED" BY HER HUSBAND

Gen. 12:10-20; 20:1-18; 1 Pet. 3:6

> He was oppressed, and he was afflicted, yet he opened not his mouth: he is brought as a lamb to the slaughter, and as a sheep before her shearers is dumb, so he openeth not his mouth. Isa. 53:7

In the Old Testament book of Isaiah, we have the picture of Jesus' reaction to affliction, of His response when He was, no doubt, "used" by His fellow men for their own purpose. How did He react? He went the way of the lamb. He opened not His mouth, for He knew that God was in control and would work things out. He did not have to take justice into His own hands.

Imagine being in Sarah's place when twice her husband Abraham tried to protect himself by telling the rulers that Sarah was only his sister! Twice she went along with the game, submitting to her husband's plan, even though it meant separation from him and hardship for her. And twice God protected her in supernatural ways, once by sending plagues to Pharaoh's household in Egypt, and the second time by causing Abimelech to have a dream concerning her, resulting in her freedom. Sarah's submission to her husband, though he may have been using her for his own welfare, was honored by the Lord. She could have refused to obey Abraham and felt perfectly justified in doing so.

She could have said, "I've left family, friends and a nice home in Ur of Chaldees to camp with you in this strange land because I am your wife. It's hard enough to believe that God would lead us into this barren country with only a promise that *someday* you would be the father of a great nation. Meanwhile, you have no permanent job, we have nothing to eat because of the famine, and I'm exhausted moving from camp to camp. Now you want to tell everyone that I am your sister! You're thinking of yourself, not me! You're using me for your own gain after all I have sacrificed for you! You expect me to become part of Pharaoh's harem, when what I've wanted more than anything else is to have children by you! Abraham, I'm sick and tired of the whole thing!" But she didn't.

Sarah's example of obedience made such an impression on Peter that he used her as an example of the model wife who even went so far as to call her husband "lord." Certainly it wasn't easy for Sarah to do what she was asked to do. Most women would have felt so "used" by their husbands that they would have cut off all feeling and respect for them.

Her secret was her attitude of submission. She submitted to Abraham "as unto the Lord." This is scriptural, for we read (Eph. 5:22), "Wives, submit yourselves unto your own husbands, *as unto the Lord*" (emphasis mine). Sarah may have lived before the letter to the Ephesians was written by Paul, but she knew she could obey her husband because she looked to the Lord for her protection and deliverance. She knew that by submitting to the authority God had set over her, He would in turn honor her obedience. She had learned the truth that Jesus revealed when He appeared in trial before Pilate and said, "Thou couldest have no power at all against me, except it were given thee from above" (John 19:11a). Once we know that all authority is from God, we can submit to man. For we realize that God has put that authority over us, and that He can also change it because He is the ultimate Authority.

Sarah had learned the secret of submission by going the way of the lamb, the Lamb who was sacrificed when He did not defend himself. In the book of Revelation, we find this Lamb reigning with God! She had learned to submit as unto the Lord; therefore, she could do whatever was demanded of her, knowing that God would reign in the end!

Dear God, my Lord, I thank you for being King of Kings and Lord of Lords, the God who has everything in control. I recognize you as the supreme Authority in my life and I desire to do everything as unto you. Help me to willingly submit to those authorities you have put over me, knowing that as I do, you will protect and guide me. Help me to know when to speak, but also teach me when to be silent. Help me, Lord, to go the way of the Lamb, to give up my "rights" for your higher plan. In the name of Jesus, the Lamb of God. Amen.

HAGAR

THE WOMAN WHO REPRESENTS THE WAY OF THE FLESH

Gen. 16:1-16; 21:9-21; Gal. 4:21-31; 5:16, 18

> Are ye so foolish? having begun in the Spirit, are
> ye now made perfect by the flesh?   Gal. 3:3

When she was over seventy, Sarah was given a word from God that she would bear a son who would inherit all the promises He had given to her husband Abraham. Since she had borne no children at all, she found this hard to believe.

So in order to make this prophecy come to pass, she gave her handmaid Hagar to Abraham that he might have a child by her. He would then have an heir. When Hagar did conceive, Sarah became so jealous that Hagar ran away. God brought her back and she bore a son, Ishmael. Thirteen years later Sarah miraculously conceived and bore Isaac, the son of promise. As these two women and the two children lived in the same household with Abraham, conflict abounded. Sarah finally asked Abraham to "cast out this bondwoman and her son" because she did not want Ishmael to become heir with Isaac. Abraham was grieved, but the Lord reminded him that the promised seed would come through Sarah, so he sent Hagar and Ishmael away. They

9

lived in the wilderness of Paran until Hagar took Ishmael a wife out of the land of Egypt.

In the book of Galatians (4:21-31), Paul gives the example of Sarah and Hagar as an allegory: living by the Spirit of God versus living in bondage to the law or the way of the flesh. Sarah was a freewoman, free to live the life of faith led of the Spirit of God. Hagar was a bondwoman, a servant; she was under the law and respresents flesh. Sarah chose to give Hagar to Abraham because, due to her age, she knew no way for God to give her a child. She chose the logical, reasonable means available to her instead of letting God perform His Word in His time and according to His will and purpose. She became as God and used *her* servant, the flesh, to carry out *her* will; God wanted to use her as *His* servant to carry out *His* will! She chose the way of the flesh instead of the way of the Spirit.

We like to think of non-believers as being under the law and living according to the lusts of the flesh. We like to think that, as believers, we live every moment led of the Spirit. But that was not so in Paul's day, nor is it automatically true in our own lives. The book of Galatians was written to a group of believers who had been given God's Holy Spirit and yet perverted the Gospel by slipping back into the bondage of legalism. They said that one could not be a follower of Jesus under the New Covenant unless he also kept the Jewish laws under the Old Covenant. Paul helped them see that this was not right. The Jewish laws had led them to Christ, but now they were supposed to live by faith, led of the Spirit, and not come under the law. They were crucified with Christ, who had fulfilled the law. They were now new creatures in Christ, free to be led of the Spirit. Paul urged them to be on guard for those times when they started out being led of the Spirit but ended up trying to justify themselves in the flesh.

Impatience is probably the single most common reason

for our fleshly conduct. Like Sarah, we are not willing to wait for God to complete His Word; we try to use a Hagar. We do not trust God's perfect timing, but lean to our own understanding.

Significantly, patience (or long-suffering) is part of the fruit of the Spirit. This attribute of God's nature develops and matures in us as we wait upon Him and as we deny our flesh.

God eventually fulfilled His word in Sarah, but all mankind has suffered for her decision to choose the way of the flesh. Abraham and Hagar's offspring, Ishmael, fathered another people, the Arabs, whose conflict with God's chosen people has continued from Abraham's day to the present.

Likewise, our acts of flesh often see long-lasting consequences. But, because we are in Christ, we are of the seed of Isaac, the promised child of Abraham and Sarah, the freewoman. We are not of the bondwoman, Hagar. Let us continually cast her out and praise God for the inheritance that is ours!

Dear God, I thank you for Jesus who lives in me, and for your Holy Spirit who has filled me. Help me to reckon myself dead to the old ways of my past and to submit wholly to your will in my life. Thank you for the inheritance I have as a freewoman in you—to be led of your Spirit even when I become impatient for you to act. Forgive me, Lord, for not trusting you. Amen.

LOT'S WIFE

A WOMAN WHO LOOKED BACK

Gen. 19:15-26; Luke 17:28-32

> Wherefore seeing we also are compassed about
> with so great a cloud of witnesses, let us lay aside
> every weight, and the sin which doth so easily
> beset us, and let us run with patience the race that
> is set before us, Looking unto Jesus the author
> and finisher of our faith; who for the joy that was
> set before him endured the cross, despising the
> shame, and is set down at the right hand of the
> throne of God.   Heb. 12:1, 2

Lot's wife is a woman whose own name is never mentioned
in the Scripture, either in the book of Genesis where her
story is found, or in the New Testament where Jesus refers to
her. She is always known as Lot's wife; furthermore, the
Bible does not record even one word that she spoke!

We can assume that she was an obedient wife, in outward
submission to her husband, even when he settled for less
than God's perfect will for their lives. When God delivered
them from Sodom just before it was destroyed, Lot chose to
go to Zoar (a "little place"), rather than to the mountains as
he had been commanded. In this, his wife said nothing, gave
no display of temper, said no threatening words.

Perhaps she could do this because she personally had experienced God's mercy, for the Lord had laid His hand upon her as well as upon Lot and their two daughters, and delivered them from the wicked city before it was destroyed.

What then was the sin which caused her death? What did she do that made God smite her and turn her into a pillar of salt? Why did He render her useless just as she was leaving the city? More importantly, perhaps, why did Jesus himself tell us to remember her?

She looked back toward Sodom. God gave the whole family a commandment when He said (Gen. 19:17), "Look not behind thee." Lot's wife was disobedient at this point and God judged her immediately.

Why did she look back? Perhaps she remembered the old life and pleasures she had left behind. Maybe she wanted just one more glimpse of all that she was giving up. It could be, too, that she was unable to go on to a new life because she remembered hurts and sins which had not been resolved. Maybe she had unforgiveness against friends, remorse at the way life had turned out for them in Sodom, or even anger at God for letting the situation there get so bad.

Like Lot's wife, we may have happy memories which we enjoy reliving; we may even wish life was like it used to be! We need to be careful that these memories do not hinder our present walk, for the Lord might want to lead us in a new way.

Likewise, we can have unpleasant memories which also render us useless to God, such as unresolved feelings of guilt or remorse. Perhaps we have felt bad about something that happened in the past even though we asked God to forgive us for whatever part we played in it. These memories plague us and keep us from going on with the Lord. These are those weights and sins of the past which "so easily beset us."

What can we do? First, we must make sure that we have

confessed our sins to God, asked forgiveness of those involved, and have accepted God's Word that, as we do these things, we are forgiven and become new creatures in Christ. We then need to ask the Lord to make those bad memories perish as we ask Him to heal specific past hurts and disappointments. He can do this, for Isaiah says, "O Lord our God, other lords beside thee have had dominion over us: but by thee only will we make mention of thy name. They are dead, they shall not live; they are deceased, they shall not rise: therefore hast thou visited and destroyed them, and made all their memory to perish" (Isa. 26:13, 14). We can also claim what Paul told the Corinthians, that when we are in Christ, we are new creatures as old things pass away and all things become new (2 Cor. 5:17).

Lot's wife did not have the benefit of knowing Jesus, but Jesus knew of her. And when He told His disciples of what would happen in the last days, He even asked them to remember her. Surely it is a word for us today as we look forward to the fulfillment of all things.

Are we, in the day of persecution and tribulation, willing to endure the cross, if necessary, and not look back to what might have been? Are we willing to be healed from all our past hurts and disappointments, so that we can be free to go on with the Lord now? Are we able to obey God's commands, even when they seem illogical?

God knew that He would be doing a special work in the end times as He uses His Body in the great harvest of souls. He knew He would need an obedient people ready to leave the past, free from worldly entanglements, and willing to trust Him when all fails. Toward that end, He asked that we remember Lots's wife.

Lord Jesus, I would remember Lot's wife. I do not want to look back to either my successes and pleasures of the past with pride or fleshly desires, or my past hurts and memories of unhappy experiences. I ask you to forgive me as I have hung on to the past by any means. Help me know your forgiving love as well as healing mercy in my life, as I also forgive myself and learn to run with patience the race that is set before me. I thank you, Jesus, that you are the Lord of my present and the Savior of my future, as well as the Healer of my past. Amen.

REBEKAH

A WOMAN WHO LET HER IDOLATRY OF A SON DESTROY FAMILY RELATIONSHIPS

Gen. 25:20-28; 27:1-17, 42-46

He that loveth father or mother more than me is not worthy of me: and he that loveth son or daughter more than me is not worthy of me.   Matt. 10:37

In the story of Rebekah, we have the frightening example of how something very beautiful can turn sour and affect the lives of many people. There is probably no more idyllic story of romance than the one found in Genesis 24. In this chapter, Abraham sends his servant to find a wife for his beloved son, Isaac. God's hand was evident as the circumstances unfold. When found, Rebekah was so excited about the prospect of marrying Isaac that she didn't want to stay home even a few days longer to prepare for the wedding! We are told that when they met and married, Isaac loved her very much and she comforted him following the death of his mother. Though they desired children, Rebekah was barren. As a very loving husband, Isaac cried out to the Lord on her behalf.

When at last the Lord allowed Rebekah to conceive and become the mother of twins, her very personality changed.

Instead of continuing to give Isaac her affection and attention, she began doting on Jacob, the second-born twin. Because he was her favorite, she began to devise ways that he should receive the inheritance normally given to the first-born son. As we read of her in Romans 9:10-12, it seemed that God knew Rebekah would do this so He could carry on His plan for mankind through Jacob, who later became Israel. God has everything in control, though He lets us choose freely. He knows us so very well that He can even predict what we will choose! He told Rebekah that the younger twin would serve the elder, but He didn't tell her that she had to deceive and connive to make that come about! She chose that way herself, and God evidently knew she would.

The twins were exact opposites, and each parent chose to love one boy more than the other. Rebekah favored Jacob, while Isaac preferred Esau. This was the beginning of the destruction of their loving family relationship. The more Rebekah idolized Jacob, the more resistance there was from both Esau, the twin brother, and from Isaac, her husband. To obtain her ambition for Jacob, Rebekah began telling lies, which led to more lies. In the process, her deceptive trait passed on from mother to son, so that Jacob is remembered as a cheater—always trying to trick others so that he could have his own way.

Idolatry always destroys relationships. When we try to make another person into our image of what we want him or her to be, we usually have to trick and deceive to make this come about. The one who is idolized is not free to be himself or herself and is put in the position of pleasing *us* instead of God. Those close to the relationship, such as other family members, often become innocent victims of tricks and deception.

Rebekah paid a great price for playing favorites with her

sons. As she tried to make Jacob into the person she desired, she lost him. To protect Esau from killing him, she had to send Jacob away. She also lost the love and respect of both Esau and Isaac in the process. Potentially beautiful family relationships crumbled because Rebekah made an idol out of Jacob.

The book of 1 John contains much about love relationships, how God loves us and how we can love others. John shows us that Jesus is the true God and the only one worthy of our worship. Almost as an afterthought, he says in the very last verse of the letter, "Little children, keep yourselves from idols." He warns us here that idols will destroy love relationships. God is the only one worthy of our full attention, and anytime we make an idol to take His place in our lives, we are in for trouble. Idolatry destroys relationships with each other and with God. It certainly did for Rebekah.

O Lord, show me the relationships which have become idols to me, and let me tear them down, so that I do not worship anyone but you. Help me to see what I do to others by putting them on a pedestal. Especially guide me by letting my husband and my children be themselves, that they may be available to you and not have to please me. And, O Lord, if I am an idol of someone, please let that person see faults in me, and take me off a pedestal, for their sake and mine. Amen.

LEAH

A WOMAN WHO WAS
NOT LOVED BY HER HUSBAND

Gen. 29:21-30:21; 1 Cor. 13:4-7

My soul, wait thou only upon God; for my
expectation is from him.   Ps. 62:5

What a spot to be in! Because Leah was the older
daughter, tradition said that she had to be given in marriage
first. And as it happened in her case, she had to be given to a
man who openly preferred her younger sister and who had
been deceived into thinking he was getting this sister until the
wedding night! How would you like to be Leah? Married to a
man who not only didn't love you, but who had already
worked seven years to be married to your younger sister!

We note in this story that the Lord had compassion on
Leah in her predicament, and He gave her many children
while He shut up the womb of the other wife. Even so, the
love of her husband never came to her.

It's interesting to see Leah's walk of faith in this unusual
circumstance by the names she gives to her children. First,
she bore Reuben and said, "Surely the Lord hath looked
upon my affliction, now therefore my husband will love me."
Like many women, she thought that having a child would

21

solve all her problems, but it didn't. Next, she bore Simeon and said, "Because the Lord hath heard that I was hated, he hath therefore given me this son also." She began looking to the Lord for a reward. After the birth of Levi, she said, "Now this time will my husband be joined unto me, because I have born him three sons." Her cry unto the Lord, which had progressed to hope in the Lord, now became praise unto the Lord with the birth of Judah, and she stated, "Now will I praise the Lord." It had taken her four sons to get to this place!

At this point, Leah's barren sister Rachel became very jealous and insisted that Jacob take her maid, Bilhah. Two sons were born of this union. Leah, again thinking that she could gain Jacob's favor, gave him her maid, Zilpah, who also bore Jacob two sons. Leah continued to name these children of her maid, saying at the birth of Gad, "A troop cometh" and at the birth of Asher, "Happy am I, for the daughters will call me blessed."

Leah herself then became pregnant again and bore Issachar, saying, "God hath given me my hire, because I have given my maiden to my husband." She had much gratefulness toward the Lord when she bore a sixth son and exclaimed, "God hath endued me with a good dowry." And that He had! She was the mother of six sons who later became leaders of six of the twelve tribes of Israel. The Lord gave her a great position in His plan for His people. With the birth of each son, her faith and hope in the Lord progressed from a cry of help to praise and gratefulness, even though we never hear of her husband loving her any more than he did at the beginning of their relationship!

Though Leah never knew the complete love of her husband, she was loyal to him and found her fulfillment in the Lord. Though she longed for her husband's total love, she learned to live not by feelings, but by faith. She accepted her circumstances and learned to lean upon God, and she did not expect her husband to meet all of her needs. She realized what every human being needs to know: that no other human being can meet our every need. We each have a "Jesus-shaped" hole inside us that can only be filled by God himself. Through it all, Leah did not become bitter; she learned to praise God in all things and He blessed her.

In our human way, we want to base marriage on romantic love. This kind of love has its place, but God has a far deeper love than we can have for one another, a love that goes beyond expecting something in return. It's a love that gives whether or not one is emotionally satisfied.

Though Jacob may have desired otherwise, God recognized Leah as Jacob's wife, and so does history. Even today, we can visit the Cave of Machpelah in Hebron and find her buried with Jacob along with Abraham and Sarah, Rebekah and Isaac.

Dear Heavenly Father, I thank you for your love which goes beyond any earthly love that I can ever know. Your love never fails; I am never disappointed, because you don't condition your love on my looks, my good works, my talents, my position, but only on your grace toward me. Help me to love others in the same way. I thank you, God, that you do not look upon the outward appearance, but upon the heart. Help my heart to be clean and pure as only you can make it. Amen.

RACHEL

A WOMAN WHO WAS BEAUTIFUL IN APPEARANCE, BUT NOT IN CHARACTER

Gen. 29:9-31; 30:1, 2; 31:19-35; 35:16-19

Favor is deceitful, and beauty is vain: but a woman that feareth the Lord, she shall be praised.   Prov. 31:30

Rachel had it made. She was physically attractive and well-favored by those around her. She had the patient love of a husband who had worked a total of fourteen years for her hand in marriage! She had two sons, Benjamin and Joseph, who became the leaders of God's people at an important time in their history. Yet all of these blessings did not give her a beautiful personality.

It's interesting how the Scripture not only mentions Rachel's beauty as outstanding, but also lists the poor character traits that were hers. What were these flaws that robbed her of true beauty?

She was jealous and full of envy (Gen. 30:1). She was jealous that her sister bore children to her husband, while she was barren. (Leah was also married to Jacob, who did not love her, but who had to marry her because she was the elder sister and the oldest one in the family had to be given in

25

marriage first!) Even though Rachel knew that her husband loved her more than he did Leah, she could not accept the fact that her sister was the one giving birth to his children. She blamed Jacob for her closed womb, a situation that didn't make him too happy!

So she strove to get what she wanted. "With great wrestlings have I wrestled with my sister, and I have prevailed" (Gen. 30:8). To compete with Leah, Rachel gave her handmaid to Jacob that they might have offspring, which Rachel could then claim as hers. She took things into her own hands to make her will come to pass.

It's interesting that James says, "For where envying and strife is, there is confusion and every evil work" (James 3:16). We know that these attitudes of envy and strife in Rachel's life led to other evil work. She deceived her husband by taking idols with her when they left Padan-aram to return to the Promised Land, and lied to her father about what she had done.

The thirty-first chapter of Proverbs gives a portrait of a truly beautiful woman. This woman is trustworthy, industrious, considerate, compassionate, wise, kind and dependable. All these worthy character traits result from a woman who fears the Lord. She realizes that "favor is deceitful and beauty is vain: but a woman that feareth the Lord, she shall be praised."

We can assume that the idols were more important to Rachel than was God—she went to great lengths to conceal them from everyone. Her actions indicate she did not fear the Lord; thus she was open to the ways of the flesh and the devil. She chose to worship idols and did not look at the envy, strife, anger, deceit, and lies that defiled her. Rachel was a beautiful woman on the outside, but she did not allow the Lord, by His Holy Spirit, to do a work inside her!

God is in the process now of making a beautiful Bride for

His Son. The Lord loves this Bride, the Church, and He wants to "present it to himself a glorious church, not having spot, or wrinkle, or any such thing; but that it should be holy and without blemish" (Eph. 5:27). We are that Bride if we are part of His Church. Are we willing to let God, through the power of His Holy Spirit, form in us all the fruit of the Spirit as He prunes away those ways of the flesh which mar our true beauty? Are we willing to let the heat of trials and temptations iron out our wrinkles caused by being too set in our own ways? Are we willing to be cleansed daily by His Word that we might be refreshed and purified? Are we willing to confess our sins that we might know forgiveness and be cleansed from all unrighteousness? Are we willing to walk in the light of truth and love that we might have fellowship with one another and with God?

Rachel's story has a sad ending. When Jacob and his family finally arrived in the land which God had promised to his father, Isaac, God appeared to him at Bethel and said, "Thy name is Jacob: thy name shall not be called any more Jacob, but Israel shall be thy name: and he called his name Israel. And God said unto him, I am God Almighty: be fruitful and multiply; a nation and a company of nations shall be of thee, and kings shall come out of thy loins; and the land which I gave Abraham and Isaac, to thee I will give it, and to thy seed after thee will I give the land" (Gen. 35:10-12). Almost immediately, Rachel, who was pregnant with her second child, went into hard labor and died during childbirth. God did not allow her to raise this boy, the youngest of Jacob's twelve sons, nor let her continue as Jacob's wife when He gave him a new name and a new blessing. Attractive, well-favored Rachel never lived in the Promised Land, for she died and was buried on the way to Bethlehem.

She never discovered the source of true beauty; she never reached the place where she could say, "Let the beauty of Jesus be seen in me."

Dear Jesus, I love you. I am an anxious bride waiting for that marriage supper when our relationship will be complete at last! Help me in the meantime to prepare myself by letting the Holy Spirit show me sins I need to confess and ways I need to change. Then, give me the strength and mercy to allow that work to be done in me. Most of all, teach me to fear you. I look forward to that great day! Amen.

DINAH

A WOMAN WHO LUSTED

Gen. 30:20, 21; 34:1-31; Eph. 2:1-7

> For all that is in the world, the lust of the flesh, and the lust of the eyes, and the pride of life, is not of the Father, but is of the world.　　　1 John 2:16

Dinah was tired of home, tired of being the only girl with twelve brothers to pester, tease, boss and use her. Though her parents, Leah and Jacob, spoiled her at times, they also let it be known, in little ways, that girls were just not as important as boys. Dinah was bored with life as it was; she wondered how the other girls her age lived. She was especially curious about life in the big city with so many more things to do, places to go, and people to enjoy. Surely, the girls there had more excitement than she did!

Early one morning, Dinah quietly left her father's drab tents and made her way to the nearby community. Fear of what might happen to her was overcome with thoughts of all the fun she would have. She began looking for girls her own age as she roamed the dusty streets. Almost immediately, however, the young men noticed that she was new in town and became extra friendly. When Shechem, the son of the prince of the country, made advances toward her, she was thrilled and made herself easily available to him.

The resulting affair between Shechem and Dinah proved to be a great disgrace to Jacob. Shechem later sent his father to her father to ask Dinah's hand in marriage. When Dinah's twelve brothers heard that she had lived as a prostitute, they became very angry and plotted a way to get even with those who had taken advantage of her. One thing led to another and soon there was a cruel massacre of many people. It had all begun with Dinah's lust for adventure which opened the door to Shechem's sexual lust toward her. She left the protection and discipline of her father's house for the ways of the world which seemed so appealing.

By definition, lust is desire, intense longing, craving. We usually associate it with sexual desire, but we can lust for many things. Lust has its roots in dissatisfaction. It wants something it doesn't have. Lust always seeks to get what it wants and usually attracts those of the same spirit, as happened in this story.

John tells us in our key verse (1 John 2:16) that lust is of the world. The lust of the flesh and the lust of the eyes are not of the Father. In the garden of Eden, Satan tempted Eve by appealing to her desire for more than she had when he told her that if she would eat of the fruit of the tree of knowledge of good and evil, "your eyes shall be opened, and ye shall be as gods, knowing good and evil" (Gen. 3:5). When Eve saw that the tree was pleasing to her eyes and was good food, as well as something that would make her wise, she ate the forbidden fruit. In the story of the temptation of Jesus following His baptism, we find Satan again trying the same method. He showed Jesus things to desire—food, power, and recognition. But this time Satan was defeated because Jesus did not lust. He was of the Father, and not of the world.

We each have our times of being a "Dinah," walking in the lusts of our flesh, seeking to fulfill the desires of our hearts in the ways of the world. This gets us into trouble time after time, because we always reap what we sow.

How can we control that lusting spirit which is in us all to some degree? Paul tells us in various letters how to deal with lust. We crucify it (Gal. 5:24); we deny it (Tit. 2:12); we flee from it (2 Tim. 2:22); and we walk in the Spirit so that the lust of the flesh won't be fulfilled (Gal. 5:16). Jesus himself told the woman at the well that whoever drinks the water that He will give will never thirst, but will have true satisfaction.

There is a little slogan which says, "Bloom where you are planted." It helps us realize that each of us has a purpose where God has placed us; He can bring beauty into our present situation. As we yield to His Spirit and find our satisfaction in Jesus, we don't need to look to the world and its attractions for fulfillment.

Dear God, I thank you for saving me out of this world, for raising me up to sit in heavenly places with you, dear Jesus. Thank you for the power you have given me over the flesh by your Holy Spirit. Do help me to be content, to not lust after those things in this world which seem so attractive and yet do not satisfy. You alone can satisfy me. I am grateful for you. Amen.

TAMAR

A WOMAN WHO
EXPERIENCED GOD'S GRACE
Gen. 38:1-30; Matt. 1:3

To the praise of the glory of his grace, wherein he
hath made us accepted in the beloved. In whom
we have redemption through his blood, the
forgiveness of sins, according to the riches of his
grace.   Eph. 1:6, 7

Tamar was the victim of much tragedy in her life. Her first
husband, Er, was so wicked that the Lord slew him! His
brother, Onan, should then have become her husband
according to levirate law, but he did not want to fulfill his
responsibility. This displeased the Lord, and He slew him
also! After this, her father-in-law, Judah, suggested that she
go back home and wait for his third son to grow up and then
he would give him to her, also to fulfill levirate law.

So Tamar went back to her father's house and waited for
Shelah to become of age. Time passed and Judah's wife died.
As Shelah became a grown man, no mention was made of
him becoming Tamar's husband. When she saw that Judah
was not going to keep his promise, she took off her widow's
garments, dressed herself up as a prostitute, and tricked him

into having a sexual relationship with her, resulting in Tamar bearing twin sons whose father was her own father-in-law as well!

Though we feel pity for Tamar because of the injustice she received in life, and realize that she had some rights according to Levirate marriage laws, we easily condemn her for resorting to trickery and incest to have the children she so wanted and deserved. Yet God's grace was great. He used this unlikely candidate, this woman with a messed-up life, to carry on the seed which eventually gave birth to His own Son, Jesus. In fact, Tamar is referred to in the book of Ruth when the elders of the land recognize Ruth, the Moabitess, as the wife of Boaz. The men said to Boaz, "And let thy house be like the house of Pharez, whom Tamar bare unto Judah, of the seed which the Lord shall give thee of this young woman" (Ruth 4:12). Ruth and Tamar, as well as the harlot Rahab, through God's grace, found themselves in the lineage of the Messiah. We probably would not have chosen any of these three women!

What is this grace of God! Whenever the Amplified Bible uses the word *grace,* it enlarges the meaning by adding, "unearned, undeserved favor and spiritual blessing." God accepts and loves us as we are. This is a fact we can hardly comprehend. Even when we say that we understand, we still try to earn God's favor and expect others to earn ours. Our human nature is to think in terms of good works, rewards and punishment, justice for all.

What does the Scripture tell us about the grace of God? We find that it saves us, it transforms us and it keeps us. "By grace are ye saved through faith; and that not of yourselves: it is the gift of God" (Eph. 2:8). There is nothing we can do to earn our salvation. We find in Romans that God bestows gifts to His Body according to the grace given each one (Rom. 12:6a). In other words, He transforms us into the people He wants us to be by the gifts He gives according to His will, not ours. Paul describes the keeping grace of God when he thanks God for keeping him faithful through all kinds of circumstances (1 Tim. 1:12-14). Most of us realize that it is only God's hand upon us that keeps us throughout life with all its trials and temptations.

God wants us to minister this same grace to others. He tells us that we can do this through our speech by edifying one another (Eph. 4:29). We also find that as God's grace abounds in us, we may abound to every good work (2 Cor. 9:8). He wants us to be channels of His grace to others because we have benefited from this "unearned, undeserved favor and spiritual blessing" in our own life.

Tamar did nothing to earn her place in the ancestory of Jesus. In fact, we might feel that she did some wrong things. But God, through His grace, chose her, made her into the person He could use, and kept her as His own. Grace is the only word that can sum up the story of Tamar.

Grace is also the only word which can sum up the story of our lives. All we have to offer God is brokenness and strife, but out of this, He can make something beautiful of our lives by His saving, transforming, and keeping grace.

Appropriately, the very last verse in the entire Bible (Rev. 22:21) ends with the benediction of God's grace. "The grace of our Lord Jesus Christ be with you all. Amen." It's His final written word to us. It sums up His story, too!

Dear God, thank you for your grace toward me, that unearned, undeserved favor that you give so abundantly. I can never repay you, but I can say "thank you." Help me know how to receive this blessing as well and learn how to pass this same grace on to others. Amen.

POTIPHAR'S WIFE

A WOMAN WHO TOLD A LIE

Gen. 39:1-20; Prov. 6:16-19; Eph. 4:24, 25

Deliver my soul, O Lord, from lying lips, and
from a deceitful tongue.   Ps. 120:2

Twice in Joseph's life, his coat was used as evidence
against him. In his youth, his eleven brothers, in a fit of
jealousy, threw him into a pit to get rid of him. When a camel
train passed by on its way to Egypt, they decided instead to
sell him as a slave. In order to hide what they had done, they
spinkled his coat of many colors with the blood of an animal
and took it back to their father, Jacob. When he saw the
coat, Jacob was deeply grieved, assuming that his beloved
son had been killed by an animal.

When Joseph arrived in Egypt, he was sold into the house
of Potiphar, the captain of Pharaoh's guard. Here he found
favor and was soon made overseer of the household. In these
surroundings, Potiphar's wife tried several times to seduce
Joseph, but he always refused her. On one such occasion, she
became very angry and grabbed his coat as he fled from her.
When Potiphar returned home, she showed him Joseph's
coat, implying that he had tried to have an affair with her.
She told this story to all the household servants as well.
Because of her convincing lie, Joseph was put in prison.

Once again Joseph was given God's favor. Joseph trusted God. He knew that even though people might have tried to do evil against him, God would always work it for good (see Gen. 50:20a). This was true when his brothers sold him to a camel train of Ishmaelites. God used this to bring him to Egypt and to elevate him to a position of authority so that he could later save his people from starvation. It was also true when Potiphar's wife's lie sent him to prison; God used him there to interpret a dream, which later led to his release and promotion to leadership.

What happened to Potiphar's wife as a result of her lying? We can imagine that she may have spent some sleepless nights knowing that, because of her lie, Joseph was in prison. Or, if she had told many lies, her conscience may have been so seared that she had no guilt feelings at all. We don't know if Potiphar's wife saw lying as a sin. But we have God's Word which tells us that lying is an abomination to the Lord and that liars will find themselves, along with the fearful, unbelieving and murderers, in the lake of fire! (Rev. 21:8).

Why is lying such a serious thing? We find that the devil is the father of all lies, because there is no truth in him (John 8:44). On the other hand, John says that Jesus is the way, the truth, the life (John 14:6). He is God's Word, and that Word cannot be broken. Simply stated, when we lie, we participate in Satan's kingdom; when we tell the truth, we are part of Jesus' way. The *Open Bible* "Cyclopedic Index" gives thirty-five scriptural references on the subject of lying. It is a very serious offense toward God; it's an abomination to Him and He has much to say about it.

Many of us will say that we don't lie—and we probably don't tell big, obvious ones. But what about the little "white lies," the ways we just let people think something is true when it isn't? Joseph's brothers didn't actually tell their father that an animal had killed Joseph, but they sprinkled his coat with blood so he would jump to that conclusion himself! Potiphar's wife used Joseph's coat to imply that he had lain with her.

Whatever the degree of lying—whether we simply refrain from telling the truth, whether we imply with our words and actions a falsehood, or whether we actually tell a lie—we are still being deceitful and are not walking in the way of light and truth which is of God. Eventually we can even deceive ourselves to the place that we do not recognize truth itself. This is the most fearful result of lying.

How do we keep from lying? We immerse ourselves in the Word of God, which is truth. Then we ask the Holy Spirit, who is the Spirit of truth (John 16:13), to show us those ways in which we do not speak truth, so that we can confess our sins and be cleansed from them. Paul tells us to put on the new man and put away lying. (Eph. 4:24, 25). We need to choose *not* to lie, as we become new creatures in Christ and seek to be led of the Spirit. With God's help, we can have victory over the devil and his kingdom of lies. We can be more like Jesus, whose way is truth.

Dear Lord, thank you for showing me in your Word the seriousness of lying. Reveal to me, by your Holy Spirit, the little ways that I lie and do not tell the whole truth. Help me to confess my sin, knowing that you have already paid the price for my sins at Calvary. I do want to follow Jesus, who is the way, the truth, and the life. Amen.

JOCHEBED

A WOMAN WHOSE CHILDREN WERE USED OF THE LORD

Exod. 1:15-2:10; 6:20; Num. 26:59; Heb. 11:23

And all thy children shall be taught of the
Lord; and great shall be the peace of thy
children.   Isa. 54:13

One wonders what went through the mind of Jochebed as
a young Hebrew mother in Egypt when she saw her own
people becoming more and more in bondage to the
Pharaohs. Here she was, a mother with small children to
raise in a country hostile to her own beliefs and background.

Her ancestor, Joseph, had previously been made a ruler
here, and during the time of great famine, had brought all of
his family into Egypt to care for them. Her father, Levi, was
one of these. But now it seemed as though they never would
be able to return to the land that God had promised her
ancestors, from Abraham, to Isaac, to Jacob and Joseph.
Times were hard and the future looked hopeless.

Jochebed had married her nephew, Amram, and they had
had two children, Aaron and Miriam. But, by the time their
baby Moses was born, a decree had gone out that all the
Israelite baby boys must be killed. With godly fear, Jochebed

hid little Moses in the bulrushes. We all recall how he was found by Pharaoh's daughter and how his life was spared. We remember Miriam's quick thinking which provided her mother to nurse the infant Moses until he was weaned. From this point on he was brought up in the palace as the son of Pharaoh's daughter.

No doubt Jochebed had many concerns for her children. Would they, too, become slaves? What would happen to Moses as he was being raised in the palace of the Egyptians? Would he forget who he was? What future was there for Aaron here in this land? Would he be forced into hard labor like the rest of their people, building bricks without straw? What influence would Egyptian playmates have on Miriam? Would the exposure to foreign culture and gods turn her from knowing the way of Jehovah?

Jochebed had no idea that God had provided that she would be the mother of the one who would lead His people from bondage in Egypt. Could she have imagined that her oldest son, Aaron, would be Israel's first priest and that her daughter, Miriam, would be a prophetess and musician, helping her two brothers minister to God's people through the wanderings in the wilderness on the way to the Promised Land?

We all have concerns for our children. We think of what is being taught in our schools and the other influences our society is having upon them. We are anxious that they have the right kind of friends and playmates. We wonder what kind of adults they will become, especially with the pressures of the world which they will have to face. We wonder how much benefit our few years of training them will be.

Jochebed feared God (Heb. 11:23). She was willing to trust Him in protecting her family, as she did what she could to raise them. Even in that, she had to entrust Moses at a very early age to other teachers. Another mother, Hannah, had to give her small child, Samuel, to Eli to train, even though Eli had himself been a poor father to his own sons.

This is all He asks of us. We must do what we can to train our children in God's way and then commit them to Him. Trust Him. He will teach them. He will save them. He will use them. And great shall be their peace because it, too, will come from God. Jochebed did this, and her children were greatly used of the Lord.

Thank you, Lord, for being the merciful Father to my children. Help me to entrust them to your care even when I can't see how they will be able to cope with all of the evil influences around them. You love them even more than I do. Give me the wisdom I need to care for them, in doing what you want me to do in raising them to know you. I commit them to you. Amen.

MIRIAM

A WOMAN WHOM GOD RAISED UP TO MINISTER IN PRAISE

Exod. 15:1, 2, 20-22; Mic. 6:1-5

> By him therefore let us offer the sacrifice of praise to God continually, that is, the fruit of our lips giving thanks to his name.   Heb. 13:15

When God delivered His people from bondage in Egypt and allowed them to wander forty years in the wilderness, He provided three key leaders for them, two brothers and a sister. He gave Moses as leader and intercessor to guide and protect them. He gave Aaron as high priest to lead them in sacrifice and in relating to God. He gave Miriam as a prophetess and as a leader in worship that they might praise Him.

God provided for all the Israelites' needs in this wilderness experience, and, whether they realized it or not, one of their needs was to praise Him! God is worthy of all honor and praise. He created all things, including us, for His pleasure. He needed their intimate relationship with Him! He enjoys worship and praise! He even inhabits it! (Ps. 22:3).

Miriam knew that God was worthy of praise. She had experienced His supernatural acts among them before and

45

after leaving Egypt. He had protected them during the terrible plagues. He had delivered them from Pharaoh's army by opening the Red Sea for their escape. He provided all their physical needs as they crossed the desert. As a prophetess, she knew God's desire to communicate with His people, and she wanted the people to respond to Him. She realized that God is in the midst of praise, and that, as they worshipped and praised the Lord, He would speak to them.

It's interesting to note what Miriam did *not* do. She didn't stand before the crowd and say, "Let us bow our heads and pray to God and thank Him for what he has done." God does hear our prayer and would have appreciated their attitude of gratefulness. Bur praying is not *praise;* Miriam wanted the people to learn to minister to the Lord in praise. So, she took a timbrel in hand and began to sing and dance before the Lord. In song, she recalled His mighty acts among them, and the women joined her in joy and celebration.

How do we praise God? If we will search the Scripture, we will find various ways, all active. We can't just *think* praise! God wants us to fully participate in worship, to minister to Him as He ministers to us. Praising God sometimes demands a sacrifice of ourselves. We don't always feel like praising: it takes too much time or energy, or we'd rather be doing something that seems more useful. But God enjoys our praise. He commands it. And we are blessed as a result.

We can, like Miriam, dance, sing, and play musical instruments before the Lord. "Praise him with the sound of the trumpet: praise him with the psaltery and harp. Praise him with the timbrel and dance: praise him with stringed instruments and organs" (Ps. 150:3-4). Sing praises to God, sing praises; sing praises unto our King, sing praises. For God is the King of all the earth" (Ps. 47:6, 7a).

God is bestowing praise in the church in these end times. It's a part of worship that has often been neglected in many churches over the centuries. We have become spectators as we participate in passive worship services. God wants us to start to praise Him now, because that is what we are going to do in eternity! All through the book of Revelation we find the elders, beasts, and others, coming before the Lord, worshipping and praising Him. In fact, John says that a voice comes out of the throne commanding, "Praise our God, all ye his servants, and ye that fear him both small and great" (Rev. 19:5). That's us! Are we ready?

Dear God, you are worthy of all praise and honor and glory and you have created me to give that praise to you. Help me to begin by faith, even when my feelings resist. I do want to enjoy your presence now and I also want to be well-prepared for an eternity of praising you! Amen.

ZIPPORAH

A WOMAN WHO DID NOT SHARE HER HUSBAND'S CALL

Exod. 2:11-22; 4:24-26; 18:1-7

Be ye not unequally yoked together with unbelievers: for what fellowship hath righteousness with unrighteousness? and what communion hath light with darkness? 2 Cor. 6:14

Behind the stories of so many prominent men are stories of heroic women. Many leaders will testify that they would not have been able to accomplish what they did without understanding and sacrificing wives. Not so with Moses. His wife was of little help to him in the call God had placed upon his life. Under the heavy hand of the Lord, he was able to fulfill his misison, but his wife was the loser.

Moses fled to the land of Midian after killing an Egyptian. It was here that God later called him through the burning bush. Soon after his arrival, Moses had gone to the well where he met the seven daughters of the priest of Midian. They had come to water their flocks, but some shepherds were giving them a bad time. Moses helped the women, who were grateful. Upon their return home, they told their father, Jethro, about Moses and explained what had happened. He invited Moses to come stay with them and tend his sheep.

While living here, Moses married one of the daughters, Zipporah, and they had two sons. We are never told much about their relationship, except during an incident when they are returning to Egypt after God had called Moses to lead His people into the Promised Land. Zipporah became angry when forced to circumcise her first-born son. She performed the rite reluctantly, blaming her husband in the process. We have no record that she actually completed the journey to Egypt with Moses.

In fact, we do not hear of her again, except for one occasion when she, with her two sons and her father Jethro, later visited Moses in the wilderness. Moses seemed glad to see them all. Jethro rejoiced for all the goodness the Lord had done for Israel and gave Moses some advice on organization, which Moses heeded. But nothing is said of Zipporah and her reaction to Moses or his situation. We are not told if she had a relationship with God, or if she identified with His chosen people. We assume she returned to her land with her father and two sons. She was a wife who did not accept her role. She did not share her husband's call.

Many women today are unconsciously caught up in the "women's liberation" spirit which is permeating our society. This spirit says that a woman has a right to be her own person, that her personal goals in life are more important than how she functions as a wife and mother. She is entitled to have her own "calling," regardless of her husband's work. Sometimes a husband's and wife's vocations will complement each other and the relationship will not suffer much. But many times it seems that when the woman puts her career first, the man ends up taking second place. Consequently he is unable to function in the proper role as provider and priest of his household.

There are also some women, such as Zipporah might have been, who do not necessarily want to pursue their own goals. They just are not interested in their husband's life and work. They never encourage him or respect his decisions. They don't teach their children to look to him as head of the household. They don't see him as the covering God has provided. They really don't share their husband's life at all.

God intended that husbands and wives be one flesh, that they treat each other as part of themselves, not as "equals," but in proper relationship to each other. Psychologists tell us that men receive much of their self-esteem from their work, while women are made to receive their self-esteem from their husbands. If a wife does not encourage her husband in his work, then she probably won't have her needs met either. He will not be the husband she really needs.

Zipporah may have been angry at God for taking her husband from her; thus she was not able to relate to Him at all. Perhaps she forced Moses to choose between God and her; in which case he felt that he had no choice but to obey the call which he had so clearly been given.

So whether Zipporah had her own goals to pursue, or whether she just wasn't interested in Moses' call upon his life, or whether she had been so angry at God that she forced Moses to choose God rather than her, we do not know. We do know that we can learn an important lesson through the example of Zipporah.

Dear God, help me to see your plan for my life, especially in relation to my husband and what you are doing in his life. Help me to be the wife that he needs to do the work you've called him to do, even though he may not be sure of this calling himself. Help me at least to encourage him, instead of being a hindrance. No matter how different our pasts have been, I know that you can mold us into one, if we are willing. Help me to be willing. Thank you, Jesus. Amen.

RAHAB

A WOMAN WHO DISCOVERED THE BALANCE BETWEEN FAITH AND WORKS

Josh. 2:1-21; 6:17-25; Heb. 11:31; James 2:24-26

> Even so, faith, if it hath not works, is dead, being
> alone.   James 2:17

Scripture admonishes us to balance our life of faith by doing works which are pleasing to the Lord. In his epistle, James gives a discourse on faith versus works. He shows how it is faith, and not our works, that saves us, as well as how faith, without works, is dead. In other words, our good works do not earn us salvation. That is a free gift of God, through faith in Him. However, once we have accepted salvation, through the gift of faith, we will want to do works that will please God.

This concept of the relationship between faith and works can be seen in the life of Rahab; she has a unique place in the Word. She is the one woman named by both Paul and James in their respective teachings on faith and works. In Hebrews, Rahab is listed in the "Hall of Faith" as one who had great faith. In contrast, James singles out Rahab as one who did good works as a result of her faith. Rahab's life can demonstrate the balance that we all need between our faith and our works.

Let's consider the story of Rahab and see why this is true.

Rahab, a harlot, lived in a house which sat on top of the wall surrounding the old city of Jericho. She probably operated this as an inn, while her parents, sisters and brothers lived elsewhere in the city.

All those who lived in Jericho had been hearing stories of the Israelities, who were coming to possess the land of Canaan. They heard how Moses, the former leader of the Hebrew people, had led them across the Red Sea. It was even said that they crossed on dry ground, while their God held back the waters! Now these children of Israel were coming close to the border of Canaan. They had destroyed the two Amorite kings. Soon, it was rumored, they would cross the Jordan River and take Jericho under the leadership of Joshua.

Many people in Jericho became afraid because they sensed the power of the God that Israel had on its side! In fact, Joshua 5:1b says that when the kings of the Canaanites heard these rumors "their heart melted, neither was there spirit in them any more, because of the children of Israel." Hearing the word about the God of Israel did not give them faith; it only produced fear in their hearts.

Rahab was different. When she heard these rumors, she had an opposite reaction. The book of Joshua (2:9-11) tells us that she believed what she heard. She decided that since this God was so great, she wanted Him for her God, as she later told the Israelite spies, (verse 11), "as soon as we had heard these things, our hearts did melt, neither did there remain any more courage in any man, because of you: for the Lord your God, he is God in heaven above, and in earth beneath." By faith, she believed in what she had heard of Israel's God.

It was simple faith, for as a prostitute, she probably felt that she could do nothing to earn God's respect. She believed because she had heard the Word, not because she had seen evidence of God. It was this faith that led her to receive salvation. And this faith came alive as she did some works.

Opportunity to do something literally knocked at her door. Two men had been sent by Joshua to spy out the city of Jericho. Whether it was because her house was so accessible, or because she made herself available, or because the Lord guided them there, we do not know. But when Rahab opened the door, they immediately asked for protection.

Even though she did not know them personally, she recognized them as Israelites and she did as they asked. It was a risk, but since she already believed in their God, she knew that He could provide for her as well as for them. And so she not only hid them, but helped them to escape safely as well. Her faith had led her to works! This brought her faith to life, and she asked for salvation for herself and her whole family. Significantly, it would be a red cord hung out of her window that would be the sign given to the Israelites to spare her house. It's by the red blood of Jesus that we are saved.

To be sure, Rahab's faith was tested. It took courage to hide the spies and to help them to safety, while wondering what her family would say should she be caught. It took trust to believe that the spies would indeed pass on the message that she and her family were to be saved, that the scarlet cord would do its job! It took patience to wait, even after the Israelites came into sight, for them to march seven days around the city without a sign of battle, let alone a victory!

Rahab passed the test. She discovered the relationship between faith and works, as she put them in proper order. First she heard the Word, then she believed. This belief led to faith, which then led to works. In the process, she was saved.

Dear God, I ask that today you show me by your Holy Spirit the relationship between faith and works in my own life. Help me to be strong in the faith, as I hear your Word and confess it. Help me to do your will that my faith be not dead. And please, dear Lord, do not let me get so involved in good works that I forget that it is only by your grace that you accept me at all. Amen

DEBORAH

A WOMAN TO WHOM
THE LORD GAVE THE GIFTS
OF THE SPIRIT FOR MINISTRY
Judg. 4:1-24; 1 Cor. 12:7-11

And it shall come to pass in the last days, saith
God, I will pour out of my Spirit upon all flesh:
and your sons and your daughters shall prophesy,
and your young men shall see visions, and your
old men shall dream dreams.   Acts 2:17

God had brought His people into the Promised Land. But
instead of them wholly following Him, they began to take on
the ways of the inhabitants and worship idols. This so
provoked the Lord that He let their enemies oppress them as
He raised up judges to rule them. Some of these judges did
evil and some did what was right and good. But it seemed
that no matter how good the judge was, the people returned
to corrupt ways as soon as he died. This turbulent period in
Hebrew history can be summed up in the last verse of the
book of Judges, which says, "In those days, there was no
king in Israel: every man did that which was right in his own
eyes." It was a sad period of time for God and His people.

The fourth judge whom the Lord raised up in the midst of
this chaotic time was Deborah, the wife of Lapidoth. We

don't know why He chose this woman or much about her qualifications except that she must have been willing to be used of God—to speak His words and do His will, not her own. God needed a leader to convey His words to His people, so He selected Deborah, a prophetess. When He gave her this special position, He also gave her favor with the people, as well as the gifts of wisdom and knowledge to lead them. She set up court in the hill country of Mt. Ephraim under a palm tree. Many came to her for counsel and judgment.

The story in Judges 4 tells how the Lord used Deborah to lead His people to victory in a particular battle. She, who knew little in the way of military strategy, passed on to Barak, the leader of the troops, the necessary wisdom and knowledge as God revealed His plan to her.

Evidently, because of this word of knowledge, Deborah told Barak that the enemy would be delivered into their hands, but that a woman would accomplish the final victory! (Judg. 4:9.) It would have been easy for her to question if she had heard the Lord correctly, but she boldly passed on the information she had been given. Deborah was willing to accept God's gifts and realize that His ways were not her ways, nor His thoughts her thoughts. As it turned out, the word did prove to be true. Through an unusual set of circumstances, a woman did wield the final blow to Sisera, the leader of the enemy troops. In seeking protection after his men had fallen to Barak, he came to the tent of Jael. When he had eaten and fallen asleep, she hammered a nail through his head!

Before the time of the outpouring of the Holy Spirit at Pentecost following Jesus' ascension, the gifts of the Spirit were limited in their apportionment to man. All through the Old Testament, we see God giving His Spirit to certain people for certain tasks, such as He did to Deborah. One time, for example, He gave to a man named Bezaleel "the spirit of God, in wisdom, in understanding, and in knowledge, and in all manner of workmanship" in order that he might "make any manner of cunning work" for the tabernacle of the Lord (Exod. 35:31, 33).

But when the Holy Spirit was poured out upon the 120 believers in the upper room in Jerusalem, the gifts were given to all those who would receive them by faith. God wanted to evangelize the world and edify the Body, and He knew this took supernatural power; He wanted all believers to be filled with His Spirit that they might accomplish these tasks.

Sometime after the early spread of Christianity, many of these gifts seemed to have disappeared. Perhaps the second coming of Jesus did not happen as soon as people expected and they became discouraged. Their faith became weak and they no longer expected the gifts. As time went on, the Christians began to think that the gifts had been given only at the beginning of the early church, just to cause the Gospel to spread from that area into all the world.

God must have known this would happen, for even then He promised that in the last days, He would pour out His Spirit upon all flesh and that these gifts would again be available to everyone. He knew that in this end time, Christians would need supernatural gifts to battle Satan in order to function as a victorious Body. These gifts are given now for the task He has for us to perform.

He may give us a word of wisdom to share with a fellow believer who is seeking guidance. He may use us to minister healing. He may give us the gift of discernment of spirits when we need to be warned in some way. He wants us to receive His gift of prophecy that we might know His will. He provides the gift of tongues that we might be edified.

God gives these gifts, through His Holy Spirit, to His Body. As we are filled with His Spirit and yield ourselves to

Him, we receive these gifts. As He gives them, He desires that we appropriate them in ministry to others. Deborah was willing to use the gifts God gave to her. Are we?

I feel so privileged to be living in these times, to see the mighty move of your Spirit as gifts are being poured out upon your Body. I thank you, Lord, that they are available to me by faith and that you can show me exactly where I fit in the Body, so that I can be a part of your ministry. I praise you, Lord, for opening my spiritual eyes and for giving me this faith. Amen.

MANOAH'S WIFE

A WOMAN WHO KNEW HOW TO RESPOND TO THE SUPERNATURAL

Judg. 13:2-24; 1 Cor. 11:7-10

> For the husband is head of the wife, even as
> Christ is head of the church: and he is the saviour
> of the body. Therefore as the church is subject
> unto Christ, so let the wives be to their own
> husbands in every thing.   Eph. 5:23, 24

Manoah's wife was one of several women in the Bible who
was barren until the Lord opened her womb in order that she
might bear the child God needed next in His divine plan. At
the appointed time, she was visited by an angel who
informed her that she would bear a son, a leader who would
eventually deliver the children of Israel from the captivity of
the Philistines.

One of the first things she did following the angel's visit
was to go to her husband and tell him what had happened.
Manoah then asked the Lord to send this man of God again
so that they together might be given further instruction. The
Lord sent the angel once more; again, the wife ran to tell her
husband. This time Manoah followed her quickly to where
the angel waited, and asked him some key questions (though

61

he thought he was only talking to a man). After this "man" ascended toward heaven in a flame from the altar, Manoah realized that he had been talking to an angel after all!

Manoah's wife did a very wise thing when twice she was visited by the angel. When the supernatural visits occurred, she immediately went to her husband for his advice. She wanted him to see the angel and talk to him, so he would know firsthand what the angel had told her, as the angel's message would affect both their lives. Whether she was aware of it or not, she was seeking to be under a covering.

Paul tells us that when worshipping, a woman ought to have her head covered because of the angels (1 Cor. 11:7-10). Some have taken this to mean that a woman should wear a hat in church. But the word "power" in verse 10 means "authority." The angels referred to in the same verse can be those rebellious spirits of Satan, as well as the loyal, ministering messengers of God. Therefore, we can interpret this to mean that a woman should be under authority when in a worship service as a protection from any evil angelic influence.

Women are easily deceived; they are easily attracted to the supernatural and may not have the discernment to know if something is of God or if it is a deception of Satan.

A woman needs protection. God knew that when He established a divine order for the church as well as for the family. The man is subject to Christ, who is the Head. The wife is subject to her husband, who is her head, and the children are subject to their parents, who are their covering in the Lord. A woman who finds herself living alone can submit to other men in her family for counsel and advice. She can submit to the elders of the Body who can test the spirits for her protection.

This is especially appropriate in this day of women's liberation. Satan is busy with supernatural phenomena, trying to deceive even the very elect. Women who seek to do their own thing are especially vulnerable to his tricks. If he can get women to assert their own rights and put themselves above God's order, he is on the way to getting them out from under the covering that the Lord has provided for them.

Sometimes women try to justify themselves and their independence, saying that their covering just isn't "spiritual" enough to understand. Perhaps their husbands are not believers at all. Manoah was not as open to the supernatural as his wife was, for even when he saw and talked to the angel, he did not recognize him as one! But when they prayed that God would show him what was happening, the Lord responded and revealed himself to Manoah. As his wife put herself in proper order, God was able to work through her husband, blind though he seemed to be!

God has a plan, an order for husbands and wives, for men and women, for parents and children. He has a divine order for the church. If we want His protection we must, like Manoah's wife, submit to His plan.

Dear God, my protector, I thank you for your super-natural protection over me from all the powers and principalities in high places. I thank you for your shed blood which destroyed all the works of the devil, and especially for your plan of protecting us as we respond to your order for our lives. Help me to know the covering I have in Jesus, as well as the covering I have in being in your divine order in my home and in the Body. Amen.

DELILAH

A WOMAN WHO PERSISTED UNTIL SHE WON

Judg. 16:4-20; 1 Pet. 5:8-10

Wherefore take unto you the whole armour of God, that ye may be able to withstand in the evil day, and having done all, to stand.   Eph. 6:13

"Samson, honey, tell me why you are so strong. I don't think anyone could ever capture you!"

"Well, Delilah, if I were tied with seven raw leather bowstrings, I would become very weak, just like an ordinary man."

With this bit of information, Delilah waited until Samson was asleep and then she tied him with seven bowstrings. But he quickly awoke and broke the strings, when he thought the enemy had come to get him.

"Samson, dear, you lied to me! You really had the strength to break those strings, and you knew it! Please, this time, tell me how you really can be captured!"

"Oh Delilah, I was just teasing; if you tie me with brand-new ropes, I guarantee that I will be as weak as anyone!"

Again, while Samson slept, Delilah tied him, this time with brand-new ropes. But once again he was able to free himself when he thought he heard the enemy approach.

"Samson," Delilah complained more loudly, "you really have mocked me. Please, if you really love me, tell me how you can be captured."

Samson told her that all she would have to do is weave some of his hair into her loom. This she did, again while he slept. However, once more he had tricked her.

"Samson," begged Delilah, "how can you say you love me, when you don't confide in me? You keep making a fool of me and still you haven't told me your secret!"

At last Delilah had worn Samson down. Her constant nagging finally paid off, and he told her the secret which would indeed weaken him. He told her to cut his hair. With persistence, she won her way.

Delilah had been used by the Philistines to defeat their enemy, Samson. In a sense, she was the Judas of the Old Testament, as she was offered several hundred pieces of silver to betray her lover. As we read the story, we wonder why Samson did not see through her beguiling ways. A man so physically strong was conquered by the enticing words of a woman!

Samson knew that God had given him strength through his long hair because of the Nazarite vow put upon him from his mother's womb. He had been commissioned by God to deliver Israel out of the hands of the Philistines. He was not ignorant of his mission and qualifications. But he did let his enemy in disguise, Delilah, keep after him. Finally, "she pressed him daily with her words, and urged him, so that his soul was vexed unto death" (Judg. 16:16). She persisted until she won.

That's often Satan's technique. If he can wear us down, he knows he will win. Finally we too will escape into sleep and let him have his way.

How can we be on guard against our enemy, Satan? We are in spiritual warfare and just the recognition of this is beneficial. We sometimes want to ignore this fact; then he has us where he wants us!

The sixth chapter of Ephesians gives specific instructions on how to be armed for this warfare. We must stand with our loins girt about with truth, while we wear the breastplate of righteousness. We should have on our heads the helmet of salvation and our feet shod with the preparation of the gospel of peace. Above all, we must take the shield of faith, along with our only offensive weapon, the sword, which is God's Word. While standing fully clothed in this armor, we pray.

Being covered with this armor and praying in the Spirit is our only defense. Even then, we do not fight the battle ourselves; we just stand still and let God do it!

Sometimes Satan wears us down by getting us to do battle in the flesh. We see people as our enemies, and we fight against them, instead of recognizing the powers controlling them. We don't take the authority given us in Matthew (16:19) to bind and loose those spirits that war against us. These are the keys of the kingdom given to the church. We have the privilege of binding evil spirits and loosing good ones. For example, we can bind the spirit of confusion and loose the spirit of peace. (We read in 1 Cor. 14:33 that "God is not the author of confusion, but of peace.")

Another way we can keep from getting discouraged in battle is by learning to praise God first in all our circumstances. When Jehoshaphat prepared to send his troops into battle, he was told by the Lord to send the praisers in first. The chronicler says, "And when he had consulted with the people, he appointed singers unto the Lord, and that should praise the beauty of holiness, as they went out before the army, and to say, Praise the Lord; for his mercy endureth forever" (2 Chron. 20:21). When they began to sing, the Lord ambushed their enemy and smote them!

God has provided ways to keep us from being worn down by our enemy, our Delilah, but it is up to us to arm ourselves with the whole armor, to take up those weapons provided for our battle, and to learn to praise Him first when we are being harassed.

Thanks be unto God who gives us the victory through our Lord Jesus Christ who is that armor for me. Lord, help me to remember the spiritual warfare that I am in. Give me the strength and patience to withstand the enemy as he would try to wear me down. Amen.

NAOMI

A WOMAN WHOM GOD
RESTORED TO ABUNDANT LIFE

Ruth 1:1-22; 4:13-17; Job 42:10-13

And I will restore to you the years that the locust
hath eaten, the cankerworm, and the caterpiller,
and the palmerworm, my great army which I sent
among you. And ye shall eat in plenty, and be
satisfied, and praise the name of the Lord your
God, that hath dealt wondrously with you: and
my people shall never be ashamed. Joel 2:25, 26

Naomi wanted her name changed. Her name meant "my
joy" or "pleasantness of Jehovah" and was appropriate in
her early life. But God had dealt bitterly with her; she wanted
to be called "Mara" which means "bitterness." (This name
probably was derived from the experience the children of
Israel had during their wilderness wanderings when they
found bitter water at Marah.) Naomi had gone to Moab
during a time of famine in her own country ten years before
with her husband and two sons. Now with the famine over
she returned home alone, since her husband and sons had
died. She said, "I went out full, and the Lord hath brought
me home again empty: why then call ye me Naomi, seeing the

69

Lord hath testified against me and the Almighty hath afflicted me?" (See Ruth 1:21.) True, she had one daughter-in-law who stood by her, but because she could not see how she would have any heir, she felt God had deserted her.

The Lord had a plan for her life which fit into His purpose for all of mankind. He restored unto Naomi more than she had lost, for He not only brought her back into relationship with her relatives, but He gave her a grandson who became the direct ancestor of Jesus, His only begotten Son. He restored unto her all the years that the locusts had eaten and gave her more than she ever dreamed of.

God is in the restoration business. He can take a destitute life and transform it into an abundant one. We have many testimonies today, particularly from young people who have been involved in drugs and immorality. We have seen how God has taken their messed-up lives and has restored them to a vital relationship with Him as well as healed them. We can look at the 36th chapter of Ezekiel where God describes seventeen ways that He will restore Israel, though His people will have been sent into captivity and stripped of all that is theirs. But God's desire is to so totally restore them that He will take away their stony heart and give them a new heart and a new spirit. Only God can do that!

So He did with Naomi. He took her back to her people, to the very ones that might have rejected her for leaving them when she did to become involved with a pagan people. At this point she probably did not care, for she had lost everything.

Here God began to put her back into right relationship with those she had left. He gave her a new heart and a new spirit as well. He used the daughter-in-law she had brought with her to restore the family that had been lost. When Ruth and Boaz had a son, which was given to Naomi to care for, the women gathered around her, saying, "Blessed be the

Lord, which hath not left thee this day without a kinsman, that his name may be famous in Israel. And he shall be unto thee a restorer of thy life, and a nourisher of thine old age" (Ruth 4:14, 15a). What a blessing! What a God that can take an empty life and restore it to a full life!

Like Naomi, He may lead us back to those of our past, but He will do a new thing. He may take us through many afflictions, but He will restore us if we will let Him. He can give us too a new heart and a new spirit!

Dear Heavenly Father, sometimes I get so discouraged because I forget that you are God. Instead, I make you human, with all our limitations. So, Lord, restore to me that faith to believe, to trust that you are greater, that you can restore to me the full life that you intended. I praise your holy name. Amen.

RUTH

A WOMAN WHO
HAD A DECISION TO MAKE

Ruth 1:6-18; 3:1-11; Ps. 32:8

The steps of a good man are ordered by the Lord,
and he delighteth in his way.   Ps. 37:23

Ruth had a choice to make. She could stay with her people in her own country and continue her life according to familiar tradition. Or she could leave her childhood home and go as a widow with her mother-in-law to live with a different people in a different country. Ruth was free to choose and the two paths led in opposite directions. How she decided we do not know, but we know that in God's plan, He provided that she be in the lineage of His own Son who would be born in the flesh centuries later.

We can think of several factors that could have influenced Ruth's decision-making:

She felt compassion for her mother-in-law who was now left alone, with both her husband and two sons dead.

She wanted adventure. She was curious to see people of the country her husband had come from.

She was not sure what she would do if she remained among her own people; perhaps they considered her different for having married a foreigner.

There is a key to the part God played in helping Ruth to make her choice; for we discover in Ruth 1:16, in her famous words to Naomi, that she says, "Thy people shall be my people, and thy God my God." Somewhere, somehow, God put the desire in her heart to choose him. In 1 Corinthians 12:3, we find that "no man can say that Jesus is the Lord, but by the Holy Ghost." The Spirit draws us to Jesus just as God must have drawn Ruth to himself. Perhaps Ruth's husband's whole family had testified to her of their God during the years in Moab, and she finally made the decision to follow Him all the way.

In our lives, we wonder how we made certain decisions. Sometimes we can see how the hand of the Lord has guided us; sometimes we think we did it all ourselves!

There are three specific guidelines which will help us make a decision. First, does our decision agree with the Word of God? Perhaps He has even given us a special word from His Word; but whether He does or not, does our choice line up with the Scripture? Ruth chose the Word of God rather than the way of the idols which had brought the Moabites under God's judgment and ultimate rejection.

Second, what do the circumstances say to us? Are things over which we have little control working in favor of the decision we think we should make? When Ruth's mother-in-law returned to Judah, Ruth had a means of travel and provided company for Naomi. She took advantage of the circumstances which had become available.

Third, do we have peace in our hearts? When God speaks the opposite of what our natural mind tells us, He gives us His peace. This is that peace that passes understanding. Ruth must have had that inner peace as she carried out the decision to go with Naomi. If she had been at all reluctant to go, she would have found ample excuses to stay with her family, friends and homeland.

These three guidelines are actually the manifestation of the trinity of the Godhead confirming the guidance. It is God who arranges the circumstances, it is Jesus who is the Word of God, and it is the Holy Spirit, the Comforter, who gives that peace.

If we will consider these three guidelines when we are confronted with decisions, and then do as David suggests, "Commit thy way unto the Lord; trust also in him; and he shall bring it to pass" (Ps. 37:5), then we know that He will help us make the right decision.

If we sincerely seek His will but think that we may have made a wrong choice, we can be assured that God will, in some way, work it for good in our lives. He gives us that promise (Rom. 8:28), which says, "All things work together for good to them that love God, to them who are the called according to his purpose." He wants to lead us. He wants us to choose Him and His ways. He had a plan for Ruth's life; He has a plan for ours.

O Lord, I am so grateful for the many ways you have guided me in the past. Many times, without any conscious awareness on my part, you were still leading the way. Help me, in the future, to trust you, and recognize that you do show me your way, even in the little decisions I have to make hour by hour. It overwhelms me to realize that you care so much for me, but I do thank you. Amen.

HANNAH

A WOMAN WHO WAS BLESSED WHEN SHE BECAME BROKEN

1 Sam. 1:1-2:10, 21; James 4:6-10

The sacrifices of God are a broken spirit: a broken and a contrite heart, O God, thou wilt not despise.   Ps. 51:17

Hannah was one of Elkanah's two wives. The lord had shut up her womb; thus, in the eyes of society, she was a disgrace to her husband. To make matters worse, the other wife had borne children to Elkanah and taunted Hannah about her barrenness.

Jealousy, bitterness and self-pity could have kept Hannah from communion with God. When these feelings take over, it is easy to be so angry at God and blame Him for our condition that we do not want to speak to Him. But the mercy of God and the love of her husband pulled Hannah from the depth of despair. The love of God poured through Elkanah as in tenderness he asked, "Hannah, why weepest thou? . . . am I not better than ten sons?"

In heaviness of soul, Hannah prayed and wept before the Lord, telling Him all her sorrows. He heard her. She humbled herself before the priest, Eli, and he blessed her.

In the process, she made a vow that if God would give her a son, she would give him back to the Lord. God granted her desire. When her son Samuel was born, she kept her promise and gave him to the Lord for His work and ministry. The Lord used him as one of the prophets to His people.

So often, in our sorrow and grief, we turn away from those who can help us the most. We are tempted to turn away from God himself, our real hope. But Hannah allowed God to work through her husband and through the priest, as well as through His own supernatural power, even though her adversary provoked her, especially at the times of the regular visits to the temple. It would have been very easy to succumb to self-pity and jealousy. Yet her habit and commitment to God kept her going.

We always have a choice when confronted with impossible circumstances. We can become angry, bitter and hard-hearted, or we can let the situations break us and fall upon God's mercy. We can cry out to Him. This pleases God, for He wants us to be dependent upon Him. He wants to be our all. He wants our fellowship. He wants the glory. Praise God for those things which break us, for we are not only more able to come closer to God, but we are more able to be used by Him as a blessing to others.

In Luke 20:18 we find Jesus saying that, "Whosoever shall fall upon that stone shall be broken; but on whomsoever it shall fall, it will grind him to powder." He was referring to himself, the cornerstone which the builders had rejected. He is also known as the rock of our salvation, the foundation of our faith. He tells us that we must allow ourselves, our will, our old nature, to break now by receiving His Word and mercy, or we will find ourselves being broken by His judgment. Either we fall upon Him or He will fall upon us.

Somehow Hannah knew that it did no good to blame her husband, to be jealous of the other wife, to fear the priest, or to be mad at God. She let her circumstances break her, and she became humble before the Lord. The Lord then honored her request and blessed her exceedingly abundantly above all she had asked.

My heart rejoiceth in the Lord, mine horn is exalted in the Lord: my mouth is enlarged over mine enemies; because I rejoice in thy salvation. There is none holy as the Lord: for there is none beside thee: neither is there any rock like our God (1 Sam. 2:1, 2) *Amen.*

ICHABOD'S MOTHER

A WOMAN WHO SAW
THE GLORY OF GOD DEPART

1 Sam. 4:4-22; Rev. 21:10-23

> But rejoice, inasmuch as ye are partakers
> of Christ's sufferings; that, when his glory shall
> be revealed, ye may be glad also with exceeding
> joy.   1 Pet. 4:13

The "glory of God" can mean different things to different
people. Simply stated, it is the manifestation of the presence
of the power and character of God. We associate it with
radiant light, celestial splendor, or that overwhelming sense
of awe one has when he knows he is in the presence of the
Almighty God.

Throughout the Bible, we read of God's glory in various
forms. It first appears in Exodus (16:7), when the Israelites,
who were wandering in the wilderness, were told that they
would see the glory of the Lord when He provided "manna"
for them in the morning. Significantly, we know Jesus as the
Bread of Life, who also comes in glory—when the angels
announced his birth to the shepherds, the glory of the Lord
shone round about them, and when He comes again and we
shall appear with Him in glory (Luke 2:9; Col. 3:4).

In the early days of the Hebrew people, God, in glory, chose to dwell in the ark of the covenant, which was usually kept within the Holy of Holies inside the tabernacle. Later this glory was seen in the temple which Solomon built for God's permanent dwelling place. Ezekiel 8-11 describes the departure of the glory of God from the temple and Jerusalem, driven out by the wickedness of the people. Before and since, there have been instances of God revealing His glory to various people in different ways. We cannot determine the manner of its appearing.

The prophet Eli had two sons who were slain in battle when the ark was captured by the Philistines. One of these sons, Phinehas, left behind a pregnant wife. Upon hearing the news of the death of her husband and her father-in-law, as well as the capture of the ark, she began labor and bore a son. As she was dying in the birth process, she named this child "Ichabod," saying, "the glory is departed from Israel." We are not sure whether she died as a result of childbirth or of a broken heart—probably both. To her, the glory of the Lord was in the ark, and when the ark was taken away, so was the glory of the Lord.

It's easy to give up and become discouraged when we don't see the glory of God. We feel that He has forsaken us, because we don't see any evidence of His presence. Perhaps we have been in situations where we really saw God move in mighty ways, and then it seemed as though things quieted down and God was very, very silent—no more instant miracles, no more exciting displays of power. His glory seems to have disappeared; we are ready to name the result "Ichabod."

God is a Spirit, like the wind which blows where it will. Sometimes God seems to remove himself from our presence. Perhaps He is testing us to see what is in our hearts. Will we, like Ichabod's mother, give up and die? Or will we believe His Word that says He will never leave us nor forsake us?

In Hebrews 11, the great faith chapter, we find a list of Bible characters who had great faith. Some of these received great miracles as a result of their faith but in this same list of the "Hall of Faith" we also find, "And others had trial of cruel mockings and scourgings, yea, moreover of bonds and imprisonment: They were stoned, they were sawn asunder, were tempted, were slain with the sword: they wandered about in sheepskins and goatskins; being destitute, afflicted, tormented" (verses 36-37). Where was God's glory for these people who also had obtained a good report through faith?

We do not see the glory of God consistently here on earth. Satan is still the prince of this world, and although God is in control, we have not yet seen the evidence of His full glory. We do have the promise, however, in Numbers 14:21, that "as truly as I live, all the earth shall be filled with the glory of the Lord!"

God wants us, as believers, to partake of His glory even now. In the last hour before His betrayal on earth, Jesus prayed, "Father, I will that they also, whom thou hast given me, be with me where I am; that they may behold my glory" (John 17:24). The more we can see ourselves seated in heavenly places with Christ and realize His unceasing presence with us, the more we can participate in His glory in our present life.

We also have a wonderful future to look forward to, as we are changed into His image from glory to glory (2 Cor. 3:18). Heaven will be all glory, for we will be in His presence! Any suffering we will have gone through on earth will be worth it when His glory will be revealed! John describes the heavenly Jerusalem in Revelation. "And the city had no need of the sun, neither of the moon, to shine in it: for the glory of God did lighten it, and the Lamb is the light thereof" (Rev. 21:23).

Glory to God in the Highest! He reigns forever! Someday, His glory will never depart! There will be no more "Ichabods"!

Dear God, I know that I cannot even begin to comprehend what the fullness of your glory really is. I do thank you for those times when you have given me even a very tiny glimpse of it. Help me to be sensitive to your presence, to appreciate your willingness to share yourself with us mortal creatures. I look forward to that day when I shall see you face to face. Amen.

MICHAL

A WOMAN WHO COULD NOT ACCEPT SOMETHING NEW

2 Sam. 6:12-23; Luke 19:37-40

And he hath put a new song in my mouth, even praise unto our God: many shall see it, and fear, and shall trust in the Lord.   Ps. 40:3

When we become "new creatures in Christ," many new things will happen to us, and we will have new things to do and to accept. Here are a few:

> We will be part of a new covenant (Heb. 8:13).
> We will receive a new commandment—the way of love (John 13:34).
> We will be given a new heart and a new spirit as God takes away our hard hearts (Ezek. 36:26).
> We will receive a new name as God recognizes us as "overcomers" (Rev. 2:17).
> We will inherit a new heaven and a new earth (Rev. 21:1, 7).

In fact, as we come into a relationship with Jesus and a walk in the Spirit, we can claim with assurance the words of the Lord in Revelation 21:5, "And he that sat upon the throne said, Behold, I make all things new!" How great are the promises to those who believe!

We have a very sad story in 2 Samuel 6 of a woman who could not accept something new, particularly a new expression of worship. In fact, we are not sure that she ever accepted her new life at all. She hung on to the old ways of her past life and was even referred to as the daughter of Saul after she had become a wife of David. Michal identified herself with the kingdom of her father rather than take on the ways and life of her husband, who would someday be king himself. It's doubtful that she ever accepted his God, and that may have been the reason she did not enjoy watching him joyfully worship the Lord. In fact, the Scripture says that when Michal saw David leaping and dancing before the Lord, she despised him in her heart!

It was a very happy occasion for David. At long last, the ark was being brought to the tabernacle which David had prepared for it in Jerusalem. Here, he and the people offered burnt offerings and peace offerings before the Lord and celebrated with a meal of bread and wine. David could not contain the joy that was his. Even as the procession moved toward the tabernacle, David began leaping and dancing before the Lord. He had the musicians blow their trumpets as the people shouted praises to God. It was a thrilling event to everyone except Michal.

Her story ends sadly. As a result of her attitude toward David and toward the Lord, God closed up her womb; she was barren for the rest of her life.

This story has a parallel in the New Testament. When Jesus rode triumphantly into the city of Jerusalem, many people shouted their praises to Him as their King. The Pharisees, however, wanted Jesus to rebuke the disciples for letting this happen. Like Michal, they did not want God glorified in a way that they did not want to participate in themselves. At this point, Jesus told the Pharisees that if these people should be silent, the very stones would cry out in praise. The Pharisees themselves would be the losers. Their lives would be barren as a result.

How set are we in our ways of worship? Are we willing to accept new expressions, even though they may actually be a return to older, more biblical forms? Do we look down on others who enjoy their worship of God?

God gives us these commandments on worship in His Word:

> I will therefore that men pray every where, lifting up holy hands, without wrath and doubting (1 Tim. 2:8).
>
> Sing unto him a new song; play skilfully with a loud noise (Ps. 33:3).
>
> How is it then, brethren? when ye come together, every one of you hath a psalm, hath a doctrine, hath a tongue, hath a revelation, hath an interpretation. Let all things be done unto edifying (1 Cor. 14:26).
>
> I will pray with the spirit, and I will pray with the understanding also: I will sing with the spirit, and I will sing with the understanding also (1 Cor. 14:15).
>
> Let them praise his name in the dance: let them sing praises unto him with the timbrel and harp (Ps. 149:3).

How much Michal is in each of us? Do we still hang on to the old ways, or will we give ourselves to becoming new creatures in Christ, participating in new ways of worship and accepting new things God has for us? The choice is up to us.

Dear God, forgive me for being a daughter of Saul, under the old kingdom of my past. Help me to accept the new life I have in you. Especially, dear Lord, give me a teachable spirit, one that is willing to learn and be open to your ways. I thank you, Lord, for making all things new in my life as I become a new creature in Christ. Amen.

ABIGAIL

A WOMAN WHO
WAS A PEACEMAKER

1 Sam. 25:1-42; Rom. 12:17-21

Blessed are the peacemakers: for they shall be
called the children of God.   Matt. 5:9

Abigail was in a predicament. The man anointed to be
king was about to meet her husband in an angry confron-
tation. In his wrath, David wanted to annihilate Nabal and
all his menservants.

Abigail's husband, Nabal, was a very rich man who owned
thousands of sheep and goats. He was also very mean and
stubborn. He acted as if he had a perpetual chip on his
shoulder, and was even more unpleasant when he was drunk.

It had so happened that David and his men had been in the
same hill country where Nabal's shepherds had been
shearing sheep. David had been kind to these men,
protecting them from harm. He expected to be able to exact
a favor from Nabal in return, so he sent some men to Nabal
and asked for food. This reasonable request made Nabal
very angry. He refused it and shouted loud insults at the
messengers. He slandered their master, David, by calling
him a runaway servant.

When David heard of Nabal's refusal, he and four hundred of his men readied their swords and prepared to murder Nabal and his entire household. Imagine Abigail's anxiety when she heard of David's plans! How could she prevent this terrible battle from taking place?

Quickly, without consulting Nabal, she loaded two hundred loaves of bread, two skins of wine, five dressed sheep, five bushels of roasted grain, one hundred clusters of raisins, and two hundred cakes of pressed figs on some donkeys. Immediately, she left to meet David before he got any closer to their property!

When Abigail, loaded with gifts, intercepted David and his men, she did an unusual thing. She approached David, prostrated herself before him, and took the blame for Nabal's foolish response upon herself, asking his forgiveness. Then she pointed out to David the problem he would create for himself if he continued with his plan of revenge against Nabal. She showed him that by shedding another's blood he would take vengeance into his own hands. She told him that God didn't want this to happen, because He wanted to give David a place of leadership as a ruler over Israel.

Whether Abigail realized it or not, she was the kind of peacemaker God desires, for she helped David be at peace with God. She knew that, to bring about real peace, she had to be willing to lay down her own life, just as Jesus did when He took our sins upon the cross that we might be reconciled to God. She took the risk of being misunderstood. She had courage to confront an angry man with his own sin and the need to be in right relationship with God.

After David listened to Abigail, he withdrew his men. He realized she was right. It takes two sides to have a battle, and when one side gets right with God, there is often no need to fight at all. This results in peace.

World peacemakers try to get people to live in harmony with one another, to recognize civil and human rights. This kind of peace never lasts, because the Prince of Peace is not in it. Without a right relationship to God, we will never be at peace with our fellow human beings. The converse is also true, for, as we come into a right relationship with God, we are more able to live in peace with others.

When the conversation with David was over, Abigail returned home. She waited until Nabal had sobered up from a drunken party, and then she told him what she had done. Within a few days, the Lord struck him and he died.

Abigail had not tried to get out of her marriage to a mean, stubborn man; but, when she became a peacemaker, God delivered her. He lifted her out of unhappy circumstances and gave her a place in God's own family as the wife of David. Jesus said, "Blessed are the peacemakers, for they shall be called the children of God." Abigail was blessed when she became a peacemaker.

Dear God, I thank you for sending Jesus to die upon the cross, to take upon himself my sins so that I may be at peace with you. Help me be a part of your reconciling ministry, helping those around me to come into a right relationship with you, that they may live in peace, both with themselves and with others. As your child, I want to be your kind of peacemaker. Amen.

THE WITCH OF ENDOR

A WOMAN WHO APPEARED AS SOMEONE SHE WAS NOT

1 Sam. 28:3-25; Deut. 18:9-14; 1 John 4:1-4

> For such are false apostles, deceitful workers, transforming themselves into the apostles of Christ. And no marvel; for Satan himself is transformed into an angel of light.   2 Cor. 11:13, 14

When one reads the story of Saul and his visit to the witch of Endor, we immediately see Saul's sins. First, he sinned by consulting a medium, after having previously put such persons out of the land. He knew that God didn't want His people to have anything to do with those with familiar spirits or who were wizards or fortune tellers. He tricked the witch by disguising himself to keep his identity a secret, and he lied to the woman.

On the other hand, it is difficult to see the witch's actions as sinful and abominable to the Lord. She didn't seem to do anything bad; she did just what she was asked. When she saw that Saul was distressed by the appearance of (and the conversation with) the prophet Samuel, whom he had asked to have conjured up, she tried to comfort him. She went so far as to kill a fatted calf and make some bread to feed Saul and his servants before sending them on their way. The witch of Endor comes out of this story smelling like a rose. She provides an excellent example of the way Satan himself sometimes appears—as an angel of light, the "good guy" who has done nothing wrong.

The witch of Endor knew who she was. In fact she reminded Saul, before she recognized him, that the king had banished her kind from the land. She knew that she was in rebellion to the law of the land as well as to God himself, because she dealt with familiar spirits. She had sold herself long ago to the devil and his way. Her allegiance was to him and not to God. *So, even though her actions appeared good, her motives and beliefs were wrong.*

We live in a day when the enemy has come in like a flood. Not only are occult phenomena on the increase, but many religious cults have sprung up as well. Some of these are exceptionally deceptive because their adherents say they believe in God, in Jesus, and in the Holy Spirit. Some have signs following them, miracles of healing, deliverance, and various spectacular manifestations of power, but they are not of God. They are of another Jesus and another spirit (2 Cor. 11:4). They *seem* to be of God, but are not.

How can we know what is real and what is counterfeit? John gives a test by which we may try the spirits (1 John 4:3). "Every spirit that confesseth not that Jesus Christ is come in the flesh is not of God: and this is that spirit of antichrist, whereof ye have heard that it should come; and even now already is it in the world." In other words, if a person or a religious group confesses that Jesus Christ did come to earth as God's only begotten Son, lived among us as that Word made flesh, then shed His blood as the perfect sacrifice for our sins by death upon the cross, was resurrected, and appeared to man in His glorious body before ascending to the Father in heaven, then that spirit is of God. Many religions agree that Jesus became flesh and lived as a human being, but do not see that this meant He also died for us. They deny the work of the blood of Jesus Christ. They don't see that it was necessary for Him to bear our sins upon His body as the sacrificed Lamb of God in order that we can be reconciled to God. They think that it was enough for Him to show us how to live while we are here upon this earth.

Bankers are taught an interesting method to spot counterfeit bills. They are taken to a place where they are given several intensive days of handling only good money. At the end of this time, their fingers can easily feel a counterfeit bill when it is slipped to them; they can now detect that the quality of the paper is inferior and that the bill just doesn't feel like "real money."

We can prepare ourselves against deception best by immersing ourselves in the Word of God and allowing the Holy Spirit to show us truth. This will help us know when the Word has been either "added to" or "taken from." Some groups feel that God has given them a special revelation, but the last warning to us in the Bible (Rev. 22:18, 19) says, "If any man shall add unto these things, God shall add unto him the plagues that are written in this book: And if any man shall take away from the words of the book of this prophecy, God shall take away his part out of the book of life, and out of the holy city, and from the things which are written in this book."

Satan is out to deceive even the very elect. He is out to trick us in every way he can, even by sending those "angels of light" which seem to be right and good. But, praise God, we have the promise (1 John 4:4), that "Ye are of God, little children, and have overcome them: because greater is he that is in you, than he that is in the world." It's by the Jesus in us, that Word of God himself, and by the power of the Holy Spirit that we will be kept from being led astray if we heed His voice.

Dear God, I thank you for sending Jesus into this world to destroy all the works of the devil. I thank you that you have given us, through faith in His Word, the power to be overcomers in the world even today. I thank you, too, for giving me your Holy Spirit to guide me into all truth to keep me from being deceived. You are, indeed, Lord of Lords and King of Kings. Amen.

RIZPAH

A WOMAN WHO HAD
A LONELY, UNPLEASANT TASK

2 Sam. 21:1-14; Ezek. 9:3-11

> Can a woman forget her sucking child, that she
> should not have compassion on the son of her
> womb? yea, they may forget, yet will I not forget
> thee.   Isa. 49:15

God's love for us is even greater than a mother's love for
her child. God has known us from the beginning and He
cares for us to the end. He is a God of love and compassion,
as well as a God of judgment.

Why is there then so much suffering in our world? Why
do innocent children have to bear so much of the pain?
These are still answers known only to God and it really
is not up to us to ask the question, "Why?" In the
beginning, God told Adam and Eve not to partake of the
tree of knowledge of good and evil. This was one thing
He did not want man to have; otherwise he would be
as a god, knowing the reasons for everything. We are to
trust Him, to obey Him, and to know that in His perfect
time He is accomplishing His perfect will. And, through
it all, for reasons known only to Him, He has allowed

man to sin and innocent people to suffer the consequences.

The Old Testament mother, Rizpah, didn't have an answer to these questions either. She didn't understand why God allowed the sacrifice of her own children for the sins of Saul. Furthermore, no one seemed to care about her predicament, much less for the dead bodies of her sons.

Rizpah was a concubine of Saul who had borne him two sons. Saul had broken an oath that had been made with the Gibeonites by Joshua not to destroy them by the sword. Then Saul died. When a severe famine overtook the land of Israel during David's reign, God showed him that the famine was a result of Saul's sin. The Gibeonites demanded that seven of Saul's sons be hung up before the Lord to stay the famine and expiate the blood of their slain. These innocent children had to suffer for the sins of their father. The two sons of Rizpah, along with five other male descendents of Saul, were killed to satisfy this requirement. When this happened, Rizpah took a lonely vigil upon the hill of execution, guarding the decaying bodies until they could be properly buried. She had to watch the blood-covered, broken bodies of the seven young men—two, her own sons—hang on trees. She saw the bodies blacken, decay and wither as she protected them from vultures and scavengers. What an experience for a devoted mother!

When David heard of her long, persistent vigil, he was stirred to remember the bones of Saul and Jonathan and commanded that they also be recovered and mingled with the bones which Rizpah had guarded. All nine sets of bones were then buried in a family grave. Her perseverance had paid off, and her sons had a decent burial.

It's interesting to note that the death of the sons, and thus Rizpah's long vigil, occurred at the beginning of the barley harvest. The first thing this woman did was to spread out a sackcloth upon a rock. (Sackcloth is not only associated with mourning for the dead as in 2 Sam. 3:31, but also with the public expression of humiliation and penitence as in 1 Kings 21:27.) For possibly six months, Rizpah kept this sackcloth in view until the rains came, a token that God had withdrawn His judgment upon the land. She also kept the birds and beasts away from the corpses as they hung upon the trees. She was not entirely passive during her long, lonely vigil.

At the beginning of the harvest time of these latter days, we are also experiencing famine and suffering of all kinds. Vengeance, which is a divine prerogative (Rom. 12:19), is, again, being taken out of God's hands and executed by revengeful men.

One can't help but wonder how many Rizpahs there are in our world today. Most of us only identify with them via television, but many are actually watching their own children suffer and die because of famine, war, poverty, and disease. Yet, we have to believe that God has known each little one from his mother's womb and is aware of all that is happening. He also knows the agony of a parent who must stand by. He himself had a Son who died a horrible death, and this Son's mother had to watch Him die, not fully understanding why.

The prophet Ezekiel was given a vision (Ezek. 9) in which the glory of the Lord was departing from the temple and a linen-clothed man with a writing kit in his hand was told to go throughout Jerusalem and put a mark upon the foreheads of those who would grieve and lament over all the abominations that would occur as that city was destroyed. These would be the ones that would have to see the young, the old, the women, and the children slain. The marking of these persons was to be done beginning at the sanctuary.

Though we do not know why these persons were marked for this unpleasant task, we observe that God seems to raise up people to be mute spectators of suffering. Perhaps in their crying and sighing, they will be repenting of sin, caring for physical needs, and standing as intercessors in prayer before God.

Rizpah's long vigil did not go unnoticed by God, and He was entreated for the land. God is aware of the Rizpahs today. And, maybe someday we'll know why they, and perhaps some of us, have been marked for this task. Until then, we trust Him.

Dear Heavenly Father, I don't understand your ways and I am easily depressed by the suffering of innocent people shown on television and in magazines and newspapers. Help me to be faithful in doing what I can to relieve the hunger and needs of these people. Help me, too, to be willing to repent of our collective sins on behalf of my country and my world. Make me a faithful intercessor in prayer. I know that you are aware of all that is happening, and I trust you. Amen.

BATHSHEBA

A WOMAN WHO
CAUSED ANOTHER TO STUMBLE

2 Sam. 11:1-27; 1 Cor. 8:9-12

> Let us not therefore judge one another any more:
> but judge this rather, that no man put a
> stumblingblock or an occasion to fall in his
> brother's way. Rom. 14:13

One balmy spring evening, Bathsheba decided to take a
bath. The evenings were long, and she was home alone. Her
husband, Uriah, had been called into battle; she had no idea
how long he would be away. As she undressed and slipped
into the warm water, she thought of how lonesome it was to
be the wife of a soldier. She longed for the day-by-day
attention of her husband.

Meanwhile King David had gone to bed, but was having a
hard time sleeping. Perhaps he had a guilty conscience for
sending his troops to war while at the same time, he stayed
home himself to enjoy the luxuries of life in the palace.
Perhaps he was remembering his close call with death in a
skirmish with the Philistines and how his men had then
demanded that he never again accompany them into battle
(2 Sam. 21:17). Whatever the reason, he decided to get up

and take a walk on the rooftop. It was always refreshing to feel the cool breeze as he looked over the city which was only part of his kingdom. As he watched the lights of the homes begin to fade, he noticed a window of a house nearby. Through it he saw a beautiful woman bathing. He could not resist the lust that grew within him, so he sent a messenger to her house, requesting that the woman come to him. She did, and the result was the well-known story of David committing adultery with Bathsheba.

We recall how, when David found out that Bathsheba had conceived his child, he sent for Uriah. He wanted Uriah to come home and lie with his wife, so the child could be passed off as his. However, Uriah was too noble a soldier. He came home, but refused to go near his wife while his comrades were at war! This frustrated David, so he had Uriah killed when he returned to battle, and married his widow after the prescribed period of mourning. God was not pleased with this whole episode, and let the baby die soon after its birth.

When we hear the story of David and Bathsheba, we usually think of David's great sins, adultery and murder. We also remember, as well, the beautiful fifty-first Psalm which details David's repentance and reveals him as a man after God's own heart.

But what part did Bathsheba play? Did she sin as well? Did her submission to David as king relieve her of any responsibility in the affair? The Word does not tell us much more about Bathsheba, except that later on, as David's wife, she had another son named Solomon, whom the Lord loved very much.

Let us, however, recall Paul's words (Rom. 14:13) in connection with this story of Bathsheba. He instructs us to keep from presenting a stumbling block or an occasion to fall in our brother's way. In other words, we should not do those things which will make another person sin, or keep him from walking with God.

We are usually aware of our witness before unbelievers, because we are anxious to set a good example that we might win them for the Lord. It is interesting to note, however, that in this verse, Paul reminds us not to cause our fellow believers, our brothers, to stumble.

How do we cause our brother to stumble? Do we make it easy for him to sin and give in to the ways of the flesh? Bathsheba did. She simply didn't bother to pull the shades. Her immodesty invoked lust in David. When he called her to his palace, she evidently didn't remind him that she was already married and wanted to stay true to her husband. In seeking to fill her own loneliness, she opened the door of sin for David. She caused her own king to stumble by her actions and reactions.

There are those today who require a certain style of dress as a sign of holiness. There are those who feel strongly about eating or not eating certain foods in order to please the Lord. Some think certain instruments are better than others for use in worship. A big stumbling block for new Christians, especially, is the growing acceptance of divorce between believers. All of thse things, and others like them, have caused division in the Body and have caused brothers to stumble. This does not mean that we do not follow our consciences and do what we believe the Word tells us to do. At the same time, however, we must not cause others to stumble by our actions or force them to see the Word as we see it. Romans 14:19 says, "Let us therefore follow after the things which make for peace, and things wherewith one may edify another." Perhaps we do have a truth, but we need to lead our brother into this truth, not cause him to stumble before he is ready to accept it. If what we believe is truly of God, then His Holy Spirit, which is the Spirit of truth, will make that truth known and confirm it as well.

David had obvious sins: he lusted, he committed adultery, he had a man killed. Bathsheba's sin was less obvious: she allowed her brother to stumble.

Dear God, I pray that your Holy Spirit may be that spirit of truth in my life today. Show me ways that I have caused others to stumble in their walk with you. Help me to find ways to edify my brothers, to build them up in the faith. And, dear Lord, show me those sins of omission in my life, ways I hurt others by not doing what I know to be right. Thank you for your faithfulness. Amen.

JEZEBEL

A WOMAN WHO MANIPULATED PEOPLE AND SITUATIONS

1 Kings 21:1-25; Rev. 2:18-23; John 3:19-21

Now the works of the flesh are manifest, which are these; Adultery, fornication, uncleanness, lasciviousness, Idolatry, witchcraft, hatred, variance, emulations, wrath, strife, seditions, heresies, Envyings, murders, drunkenness, revellings, and such like: of the which I tell you before, as I have also told you in time past, that they which do such things shall not inherit the kingdom of God.   Gal. 5:19-21

Jezebel was a wicked, domineering woman. She was the daughter of Ethbaal of Zidon, who was both king of that land and priest of Baal. Somehow, somewhere, she met and married Ahab, King of Israel, who (according to 1 Kings 16:30) "did evil in the sight of the Lord above all that were before him!" What a combination they made!

It was a disastrous union for the people of Israel. Not only did Jezebel encourage Ahab in idol-worship, but she manipulated him as she sought to rule the kingdom herself. Even the prophet Elijah feared her. Once, he and the other prophets of God hid themselves in a cave to escape her wrath. The historian describes the rule of Ahab: "But there was none like unto Ahab, which did sell himself to work wickedness in the sight of the Lord, whom Jezebel his wife stirred up" (1 Kings 21:25).

One of the stories illustrating Jezebel's power to "stir up" is found in 1 Kings 21. It tells about a man named Naboth who had a vineyard on the outskirts of the city, near the king's palatial grounds. Ahab wanted to buy this land and when Naboth refused to sell it to him, Ahab became sullen and depressed. When he told Jezebel what had happened, she immediately determined to get the vineyard at any cost. So, behind Ahab's back, she sent letters in his name to the civic leaders of Jezreel, demanding that they summon Naboth and accuse him of cursing God and the king. At the same time, she arranged to have false witnesses testify to this fact. As a result, Naboth was stoned to death and the vineyard became Ahab's.

The Lord's wrath was stirred, however, and He sent Elijah to Ahab to tell him that he would be killed to avenge the blood of Naboth, and because he had sold himself to the devil, he and his descendents would be forever cursed. God also said that Jezebel would die a horrible death and her body would be eaten by dogs.

We have an interesting description of this power of Jezebel to "stir up" when Joram said to Jehu, "What peace, so long as the whoredoms of thy mother Jezebel and her witchcrafts are so many?" (2 Kings 9:22b). We usually think of witchcraft in association with Satan's rule. Witches call upon his power to exercise their power, and Satan uses witches to perform his supernatural acts. Jezebel, as a pagan idol-worshipper, may have, indeed, called upon the power of her gods to accomplish her will.

However, Paul gives "witchcraft" another definition in

Galatians. He calls it a work of the flesh, which is in opposition to the fruit of the Spirit. God wants to shape us into His image as we yield to the leading of His Holy Spirit. He wants to produce His fruit, His nature, in us. Often, however, our flesh rises up and wants to control things. If we allow this soulish power to take over, we will usually get our way, even if it means scheming, lying, and manipulating people and situations. We will set up circumstances, as Jezebel did, to force people into doing our will. As we use that power of the flesh within us, we are using witchcraft, even as a witch calls upon a power other than God himself to perform a task. We become *as* God, instead of yielding ourselves *to* Him and letting God's Spirit control us.

Often we do this unconsciously, as habits learned from childhood. Perhaps, at that time, we threw a temper tantrum to get our way. In our teen years, we probably told our parents only what we wanted them to know, so that circumstances would work in our favor. We came to adulthood already skilled in setting up circumstances to get our children, our husbands, and our friends to do what we want them to do. Manipulating people and controlling situations are almost second nature to us. In fact, it is part of that old nature within us that needs to die!

Galatians 5:20-21 says that those who do this work of the flesh, the witchcraft, will not inherit the kingdom of God. Why? Because God's kingdom is light and truth and love. Witchcraft does not function in these; it must have darkness, deception, and the absence of true love. When we manipulate people, we do not walk in the light, and we often withhold the whole truth. This is not God's love; we love ourselves more than Him or others.

Jezebel performed more works of the flesh than possibly any other woman in Scripture, but witchcraft was one of her most outstanding sins. The book of Revelation warns about her type of person, one who seduces the saints. We are to beware of this trait in others, as well as in ourselves, lest we too find ourselves participating in Satan's kingdom of darkness instead of God's kingdom of light. We must learn to deal with our flesh, particularly the subtle work of witchcraft.

Dear God, forgive me for the many times I both consciously and unconsciously scheme to get my way. Forgive me for trying to make people into my image instead of letting them be led of your Spirit. I ask your Holy Spirit to be that spirit of truth in my life to show me where I operate in darkness. Thank you, Lord, for helping me to be a child of light and thus a part of your kingdom. Amen.

THE WIDOW OF ZAREPHATH

A WOMAN WHO HELPED ANOTHER OUT OF HER OWN GREAT NEED

1 Kings 17:8-24; Luke 4:25, 26; Phil. 4:15-19

> But whoso hath this world's good, and seeth his brother have need, and shutteth up his bowels of compassion from him, how dwelleth the love of God in him?   1 John 3:17

Jesus felt the rejection of His own people as He taught in the synagogue in his hometown of Nazareth. He reminded them that God will use even Gentiles (or foreigners) to carry out His plan if His own people will not listen to Him and obey Him. He recalled two Old Testament stories showing how this actually happened. One of these stories told of the widow of Zarephath, to whom God sent Elijah during a time of great famine in the land of Israel. God used her to feed and care for His great servant.

When we read the story of Elijah and this widow in 1 Kings, we find the woman gathering sticks, getting ready to make herself and her only son one last meal before they died of starvation. She must have been tempted to keep what she had, to make it last as long as possible. Yet, somehow, when Elijah arrived in her city, the Lord had already prepared her

her heart to receive him. For, when he asked the widow to share the meal with him, she was willing to do as he asked, even though she did not know who he was.

She didn't have a barrel full of meal and a cruse full of oil with which to feed him. Rather, she had just the exact amount of meal and oil to prepare one more meal. She had to wholly depend upon the Lord as He spoke through Elijah, and she prepared that meal by faith. She gave to Elijah out of her real need.

It's easy to think that when we have a little extra money, we will give to some worthy cause, whether a Christian organization or an individual in a financial crisis. Or we think that when we have more time, we will minister to those people God puts into our lives. We always want the assurance of an abundance—whether it be money, time, or talent—before we give to someone else. Yet, that is not God's way. He says in Luke 6:38, "Give, and it shall be given unto you; good measure, pressed down and shaken together, and running over, shall men give into your bosom. For with the same measure that ye mete withal it shall be measured to you again." We give and then we receive. We seek first the kingdom of God and His righteousness, and then our needs will be taken care of. We have to make the first move by faith.

Then too, God doesn't always respond exactly as we expect. As the widow of Zarephath gave of her oil and meal to make cakes for Elijah, God replenished the supply exactly, not one extra spoonful of meal or one drop of oil. Her obedience by faith in this area, which did not produce lavish results, led to an abundance of mercy when she had another need. Her son became very ill and died. Because Elijah happened to be there, he was able to pray that the boy might live again. God answered this prayer and the boy came back to life, and she gave God the glory. In the first need,

God simply provided as she gave; in the second, He abundantly supplied in much greater proportion than she could ever give. The grace of God dictates that He gives to us, not because we are worthy, but because He wants us to show His mercy and demonstrate the giving spirit that He has toward us.

The widow of Zarephath did not know how God would respond as she stepped out in faith to give. She simply did as she was asked, and the Lord provided. She learned to give in faith without seeing the results first. She trusted God, even when she was asked to give at a time when it seemed others should be giving to her. She had learned God's secret of giving and receiving.

Dear God, I don't know why it is so hard to keep having faith in your provision, especially when you send some situation into my life to test my faith. I do thank you that you know me better than I know myself, and that it is really only by your mercy that you allow me to keep stepping out in that small bit of faith and keep helping me to cook that one more meal with no more food in sight. Thank you, too, for those many ways you do provide which I often take for granted. I am grateful. Amen.

THE WIDOW WITH
THE POT OF OIL

A WOMAN WHO WAS REWARDED
FOR HER OBEDIENCE

2 Kings 4:1-7; Matt. 14:15-21; 1 Cor. 1:27-29

> But God hath chosen the foolish things of the
> world to confound the wise; and God hath
> chosen the weak things of the world to confound
> the things which are mighty.   1 Cor. 1:27

This widow needed help. Her husband had been one of the sons of the prophets, a group of men that the prophet Elisha had taught. She had no money to pay the debts left her following her husband's recent death, and the creditors had already come and asked for her two sons as slaves to satisfy the debts.

When she sought Elisha's advice, he gave her some unusual commands. First, he told her to go to all her neighbors and borrow every empty vessel she could get. Next, he told her to go home and shut the door. Then, he told her to take the one pot of oil that she had, and pour the contents into the containers which she had borrowed. When she and her sons did this, the oil multiplied until every vessel was filled! She was then able to sell the oil and pay her debts.

The amazing thing is that this woman did exactly as she was told. The Lord rewarded her obedience with a miracle comparable to Jesus' taking the five loaves and two fish to feed the multitude. She could have said, "This doesn't make any sense! I don't see how collecting empty jars from the neighbors will help pay my debts. And if I am supposed to sell oil to get some money, wouldn't it be better if they just gave me pots full of oil already? Besides, what's to be gained by going home and doing all of this behind closed doors? If God was going to perform a miracle, wouldn't He want everyone to see it happen?" Yet, she obeyed Elisha's instructions down to the last detail.

All through biblical history, we have examples of people who were rewarded for their obedience to the Lord, even though they were asked to do some seemingly foolish things.

With no water in sight, Noah was asked to build an ark. "Thus did Noah; according to all that God commanded him, so did he" (Gen. 6:22).

Abraham, who had no children and lived in a pagan land, was told to leave his country and all his kinsmen and to go to a new land where he would become the father of a great nation. He obeyed. "Abram departed, as the Lord had spoken unto him" (Gen. 12:4).

Elijah, during a time of great famine, was told to go to a brook, where God had commanded ravens to feed him. "So he went and did according unto the word of the Lord" (1 Kings 17:5).

Naaman, captain of the host of the king of Syria, was healed of leporsy when he dipped himself seven times in the Jordan River at the word of the Lord from Elisha (2 Kings 5).

When Peter needed money to pay taxes, Jesus told him to cast his hook into the sea. When he did this, Peter found the money he needed in the mouth of the first fish he caught (Matt. 17:27).

Paul received his sight back when a man named Ananias came to see him as directed, following Paul's encounter with the Lord on the road to Damascus (Acts 9:17, 18).

God uses these seemingly foolish actions on the part of men to accomplish His divine will. Paul summed it up (1 Cor. 4:10) when he said, "We are fools for Christ's sake."

What are some of the things we as His followers are told to do in the Word that may seem foolish to the world?

When we are sick, James says, "Let him call for the elders of the church; and let them pray over him, anointing him with oil in the name of the Lord: And the prayer of faith shall save the sick, and the Lord shall raise him up; and if he have committed sins, they shall be forgiven him" (James 5:14-15).

When others are sick, Mark gives us these instructions: "And these signs shall follow them that believe . . . they shall lay hands on the sick, and they shall recover" (Mark 16:17-18).

If we want to find life, we must lose it (Matt. 10:39).

If we desire freedom from anxiety about what we shall eat, where we shall live, or what we shall wear, we must seek first God's kingdom and His righteousness (Matt. 6:31-34).

What does God really want from us? He wants our complete obedience; He wants us to be more willing to follow Him than to be afraid of what others think. God wants us to follow Him with our whole hearts. He wants us to trust Him in whatever He asks us to do. Like the widow in this story, He wants us to do exactly as He commands, whether it seems foolish or not. Only then will we be fully blessed.

Dear Lord, I thank you for that faith only you can give me to wholly follow you. Even though I desire to do your commands, I realize that it's only by your grace and power that I am able to carry them out. Oh, God, I can't comprehend your ways, nor your love to me, but I thank you. Amen.

THE SHUNAMMITE WOMAN

A WOMAN WHO PERSEVERED IN CLAIMING GOD'S WORD

2 Kings 4:8-37; 8:1-6; Mark 11:23, 24

> The grass withereth, and the flower thereof
> falleth away: But the word of the Lord endureth
> for ever.   1 Pet. 1:24b, 25a

The Second Book of Kings contains a very interesting story about a woman of Shunem and her relationship with Elisha, a prophet of God. As the story unfolds, we find her inviting Elisha into her home to eat bread. This got to be a habit, and during this time, she perceived that he truly was a man of God. After consultation with her husband, she had a room built for Elisha to stay in whenever he came through the area. Their friendship grew.

Though she asked for nothing in return, Elisha wanted to bless her for her provision; so, when he discovered from his servant that she longed for a child, he told her that she would have a son. In due time, a son was born to her, but several years later, tragedy struck and this child of promise became ill and died. Elisha was not there when this happened, and the Shunammite woman felt compelled to find him, tell him what had happened and remind him that he had promised her this child. She would take no substitute for Elisha's presence, so he returned with her. Calling upon God's wisdom and power, Elisha was used of the Lord to restore the boy to life again.

Some time later, Elisha warned her of an approaching famine. She took her household, left the country, and found protection. When she returned to her land following the famine, she cried out to the king for her house and her land, and the king restored to her all that was hers. Whatever the problem, she prevailed upon Elisha or the king until she got an answer. She did not let the promises made to her slip away.

In this meditation concerning this woman, let us think of her relationship with Elisha as an analogy of our relationship with the word of God in our lives. We are the woman of Shunem; Elisha represents God's written word to us.

First, we note that the relationship began casually, but, as they met often, the woman began to see that Elisha was truly a holy man of God. It was then that she wanted to prepare a place where he could stay in her home, for she was desirous of a continuing relationship with him. Although she asked for nothing, Elisha gave her a promise. This promise was fulfilled, but suddenly it was gone. She had a choice: she could sit down in despair and become bitter toward Elisha, or she could remind him of the promise he had made and claim it for her own. She chose the latter, although she had to watch her tongue. Many around her wanted her to confess the problem, but her only response was, "It shall be well." She hung on by faith even when the circumstances looked grim. When she reached Elisha, the source of the promise, she reminded him that she had told him she didn't want to be deceived. She would not give up until he returned with her to fulfill his word, for she knew his word was God's word and it would not return void. When the miracle did, indeed, take place, the woman of Shunem bowed herself to the ground as she took up her son, alive and well once more. She gave God the glory for fulfilling His word in her life.

Claiming a promise from God's Word is not always easy. It's not that God doesn't mean what He says, but we sometimes forget that we have a part in realizing the fulfillment of it.

What were some of the things the woman of Shunem did to claim the word for herself? What are some of the things we must do if we want to see God's word come true in our own lives?

She prepared a place for a continuing relationship with Elisha; we can prepare our hearts for continual communion with God in His Word.

When circumstances seemed to disprove the promise, she didn't give in to despair or negative confession; we can confess the Word, instead of the problem.

She went to the source of the promise and was persistent until Elisha restored the word he had given; we can stand on God's Word, claiming it with patience, until He brings it to pass.

She accepted no substitute for Elisha himself; we can look to God and His Word for fulfillment and not accept shortcuts devised by man.

When her son was restored to life, she first bowed to the ground; when the promise in His Word is fulfilled in our lives, we can give God the glory.

Dear Heavenly Father, I thank you for sending Jesus, the Word, into our world to become flesh among us. Thank you, too, for your written word which can also become real in our lives even today. Help me to believe your word and to claim it as my own, even when it appears not to be true for me. I trust you. Amen.

NAAMAN'S WIFE'S MAID

A YOUNG WOMAN
WHO SHARED HER FAITH
2 Kings 5:1-19; Matt. 5:14-16

But ye shall receive power, after that the Holy
Ghost is come upon you: and ye shall be
witnesses unto me both in Jerusalem, and in all
Judea, and in Samaria, and unto the uttermost
part of the earth.   Acts 1:8

Naaman was a great man. He was captain of the Syrian
army and had led his troops to many glorious victories. He
was a mighty man of valor, but tragedy had befallen him—
he had become a leper.

On one of his excursions into Israel, he had taken captive
a young Hebrew maiden whom he brought home to serve
his wife in their fine home. The Word gives no more
information about her, but we can assume that she
was frightened from being suddenly uprooted from
her family and friends, as well as taken from her country
with all its traditions and culture. She was a stranger
in a strange land. She probably was not used to such
great wealth, nor accustomed to the ways of this new
household. It would have been easy for her to withdraw from

normal conversation, let alone give a testimony to her own faith.

She, however, accepted her circumstances and was friendly with her mistress. And, when she heard of this woman's concern for her husband and his illness, the young maid felt great compassion. She wanted to help him, and she knew where he could get the healing he so badly needed. She told the wife, who then told her husband, that there was a prophet in Samaria who performed many miracles, including healing.

Arrangements were then made for Naaman to visit Elisha, which he did. We recall how Elisha, through his servant, asked Naaman to dip himself seven times in the Jordan River. At this request, Naaman became very angry. Then, a servant reminded him that if he had been asked to do some great thing, he would have done it! So, Naaman humbled himself and did as he was asked, the result being that not only was he healed from leprosy, but he came to believe in the God of Israel as well. The Lord had used a young Hebrew maid to bring a great man of Syria to himself.

It's scary to think what would have happened had the maid not given testimony to her faith. Not only would Naaman have missed being healed; but many people may not have found the Lord.

There are times in each of our lives when God puts us in a "Syrian household," where we are the only one who knows the answer. It's easy to say "people wouldn't understand," "their need is none of my business," or "I am only a little maid compared to those around me." Yet we may be the only one available for God to use. Are we willing to be His witnesses, no matter what the circumstances?

We may be the only one today who can write an encouraging letter to a friend who is going through a divorce. We may be the only one in our neighborhood who knows the heart-cry of a particular young mother, hassled all day long with young children. Perhaps we are the only one who can share Jesus with a certain lonely woman sitting on the park bench. We may be the only one aware of the need to share the Word of comfort and healing with a fellow sister in the Lord. We may be the only one willing to pray with a fellow employee who has a special need in her life. We, like Andrew with Simon Peter, may be the very one God will use to bring a member of our family to Him. We are indeed the one God has chosen to be the mother of our children and the wife of our husband, and every day there are ways we can minister to them.

Are we ready at all times to share our faith—to tell others how God can help them, too? Are we willing to speak up for the Lord, even when we are not in our normal surroundings? Will we let God use us today, as He did the young maid in Naaman's household?

Dear Father in heaven, I am humbled to realize that you cared enough for me to send someone into my life to share the Good News of salvation, as well as those who have comforted me and helped me in my walk of faith. Let me, today, be your witness, your messenger to just the person you have selected. And, in this, help me to be led of your Spirit. Amen.

HULDAH

A WOMAN WHO WAS
CAREFUL IN HER SPEECH
2 Kings 22:8-20; Eph. 4:25-5:6; James 3:1-2

Set a watch, O Lord, before my mouth; keep the
door of my lips.   Ps. 141:3

Josiah reigned for thirty-one years in Jerusalem. Though
he was only eight years old when he became king, he is
known as one of the few good kings of Judah. He wanted to
please God, so he called for many reforms, one of which was
the project of repairing the temple. While this was taking
place, Hilkiah, the high priest, found an old book of the law
which he gave to king Josiah. When the king heard the words
of this book, he rent his clothes as he realized how much his
nation had strayed from God's plan for them. He knew that
God's wrath would be upon them because of their rebellion
and disobedience. He called the priest, a scribe, and some
servants, and asked them to somehow inquire of the Lord to
find out what they should do now. This was quite an
assignment! Where would they go for such an answer?

They could have gone to Jeremiah, as he had begun his
ministry as a prophet of God during Josiah's thirteenth year
as king. But, for some reason, they decided to go to Huldah,

a prophetess, who lived in Jerusalem with her husband, Shallum, keeper of the royal wardrobe. Maybe she was closer at hand and they wanted a speedy answer. She was known as a true prophetess, one who spoke for the Lord. She had to be careful to hear correctly from God, as well as in what she told the people. She knew the awesome responsibility of conveying God's words to His people. Now she was faced with the task of hearing what God wanted to say to the king.

As it happened, her prophecy proved true once again. She told the messengers that, though God would surely punish His people for their rebellion, He would also allow King Josiah to die in peace because of his humility and desire to follow Him. These were not easy words to speak, for they were not what the people wanted to hear.

We may not be recognized as prophetesses of God, as was Huldah, but we all should desire to speak His truth as He reveals it to us. We all need to say what He wants us to say. We can all learn to watch our speech, to ask the Lord to guard our lips and mouth that we might speak only what is pleasing to Him.

Paul has much to say about our communication with one another (Eph. 4:25-5:6). Here he reminds us that we should not lie, speak evil, speak in anger or bitterness, use filthy words, talk foolishly, or even to jest! Rather, we should use words that will edify one another.

In the book of James, the whole third chapter is devoted to the subject of the tongue and how it can be used for good or for evil. Verse 10 says, "Out of the same mouth proceedeth blessing and cursing. My brethren, these things ought not so to be." Our tongue, even though it is a little member of our body, can defile the whole body. We can speak unkind, accusing words, words that leave others wounded for a long time. Sometimes, we even intend to hurt people by what we say, in order to seek revenge. Or we can choose to speak words of encouragement, comfort, and blessing. We decide what we will say.

A more subtle misuse of the tongue is described (1 Tim. 5:13) in an admonition to young widows on the use of their time. Paul says, "And withal they learn to be idle, wandering about from house to house; and not only idle, but tattlers also and busybodies, speaking things which they ought not." This is just plain gossip, of which many of us women are guilty! It is even more frightening to read (Matt. 12:36, 37) that "every idle word that men shall speak, they shall give account thereof in the day of judgment. For by thy words thou shalt be justified, and by thy words thou shalt be condemned." We will have to answer for every word that we speak!

What can we do? First, we need to repent of those things which we have said that were wrong, whether we said them intentionally or unintentionally. We need to ask forgiveness where we know someone is hurting because of our words. Then, we need to ask the Lord to change our hearts; for if our hearts are full of evil, we will speak evil. Jesus reminds us in Matthew 12:34 that it is out of the heart that the mouth speaks. We need to ask the Lord to show us the anger, bitterness, and resentment that may be keeping us from speaking good things.

It's significant that our tongue is affected when we come into the baptism in the Holy Spirit. We speak in a new tongue. God, at last, has some control of the unruly member of our body. 1 Corinthians 14:4a tells us that, as we speak in this new tongue, we speak words that *He* has put in us, thus edifying or building ourselves up. A tongue which has been used for evil can, with the help of the Holy Spirit, be used to speak good. We are built up in the Lord by the Holy Spirit who speaks through us: Our words can become God's words.

It takes discipline on our part to learn to yield to the Holy Spirit, to know what He would have us say. It takes patience to study and meditate upon God's written Word so that we may speak it at the appropriate time. It takes determination of our will to choose to bless instead of curse. It takes courage to confess God's Word when the world is expecting us to confess Satan's words.

God spoke through Huldah because she carefully watched her words, and thus became that vessel of communication that He could trust with His word. We can be too.

Dear God, I do ask you to forgive me for the unkind, idle words that I have allowed to come out of my mouth. Please change my heart so that I may have the right thoughts before I speak. I thank you for your Holy Spirit who helps me to speak those things that are pleasing to you, whether in a language that my fellow men can understand, or in a tongue that only you know. Help me to realize the importance of words and to speak ones that can be trusted. Amen.

THE QUEEN OF SHEBA

A WOMAN WHO WAS REWARDED
IN HER SEARCH FOR WISDOM

2 Chron. 9:1-12; Matt. 12:42

> If any of you lack wisdom, let him ask of God,
> that giveth to all men liberally, and upbraideth
> not; and it shall be given him.   James 1:5

Over hundreds of miles of dusty trails from a city in what
is now Saudi Arabia, the camel train made its way to the city
of Jerusalem. It traveled slowly, for the animals were heavily
laden with rare spices, precious stones, and an abundance of
gold. The Queen of Sheba was on a mission, giving of her
time, her possessions, and her own life to make this most
difficult trip. She had heard of the great wisdom of Solomon
and was determined to find out for herself if all the glowing
reports were true.

When she reached Jerusalem, she was invited to tour the
palace ground, to observe the royal attendants and their
apparel, and eat at the king's table. Everything she saw
simply confirmed all the rumors she had heard. She was,
indeed, greatly impressed.

She had not come just to see all of this grandeur, however.
After all, she was a queen in her own country and also

129

possessed much wealth. When her visit was over, she presented to Solomon many luxurious gifts, and even gave him some treasures that he did not have! The Queen of Sheba's one desire was to see and hear for herself the great wisdom of Solomon.

She spent much time grilling him with hard questions, asking him "of all that was in her heart." In return, he answered every question with profound wisdom. She was so thrilled with what she saw and heard, commenting that one half of the greatness of his wisdom had not been told her. Everything exceeded the fame of which she had heard! She, the queen of a pagan country, had come to see what wisdom the God of Israel had given to His king Solomon. Although we do not know whether she accepted Jehovah as her Lord, she did bless the God of Israel, whom she believed must have been delighted to have a king such as Solomon to whom He could impart such wisdom.

Many centuries later, Jesus reminded the scribes and Pharisees of this queen who had traveled so far to see Solomon and to behold his wisdom. He reminded them that she had sought the wisest and most wonderful teacher she knew. She was willing to make a long, tiring journey to receive this wisdom for herself. He told them that one greater than Solomon was in their midst, implying that He, Jesus, was Wisdom incarnate. Because they were not willing to accept Him and all He could give them while He was with them, they were the losers.

How do we today get the wisdom we need in our own lives? Who has the answers we need for the decisions we must make? Where can we go for help?

A trap many people fall into is seeking wisdom and knowledge from horoscopes, fortune tellers, astrologists, or by other occult means. God repeatedly warns us throughout the Bible that we should not turn to these sources for answers, since they are of Satan. They are his means of giving people false wisdom. And he will try every way he can to deceive us, make us afraid, and discredit God.

We discover (Col. 2:3) that in Jesus are hidden all the treasures of wisdom and knowledge. He is the source of all true wisdom. We know from James that the wisdom that comes from heaven is "first of all, pure; then peace loving, considerate, submissive, full of mercy and good fruit, impartial and sincere"(James 3:17, NIV). These attributes, of course, describe Jesus' nature.

How do we receive such wisdom? We read God's Word and obey it. For, as Jesus is the Word of God, He is also the Wisdom of God. We can ask God for specific wisdom and He, through His Holy Spirit, will guide us into truth and its application. One of the gifts of the Holy Spirit is the word of wisdom (1 Cor. 12:8). We must look to Jesus, for in Him are all wisdom and all knowledge. Unlike the Queen of Sheba, we do not have to go very far to find wisdom; we can have the mind of Christ when we accept Jesus into our hearts. His wisdom then dwells in us as we abide in Him. Wisdom, for us, is only a prayer away.

Dear God, I thank you for Jesus, for in Him we have all wisdom and knowledge. Help me to remember to ask for this wisdom that I know you want to give me. There are so many times when I just don't know what is best in certain situations, or how to answer questions put to me, or what to say to people filled with unbelief. Father, I need your wisdom all day long. Thank you for the Holy Spirit who reveals this wisdom to me. Amen.

QUEEN VASHTI

A WOMAN WHO
DISOBEYED AUTHORITY
Esther 1:1-2:1; 1 Tim. 4:1-6

> Then Peter and the other apostles answered and
> said, We ought to obey God rather than
> men.   Acts 5:29

Queen Vashti was the wife of Ahasuerus, a man of
great wealth and fame. As King of Persia, he ruled over
127 provinces from India to Ethiopia. In the third year of
his reign, he held a great celebration which lasted 180
days. To this great display of wealth and glory of his
empire, he invited all the nobles and princes of the
provinces. When it was over, the king gave a special
week-long party for all those who had helped to make
the celebration such a success. On the last day of this
revelry, when he was drunk with much wine, he commanded
that Vashti be brought in to this gathering for all the men to
see. She was a beautiful woman, and, as a climax to the
whole celebration, he wanted to show her off. But Queen
Vashti chose not to submit to his demand. As a result,
Ahasuerus became very angry with her, so angry, in fact,
that he decreed that her royal estate be taken from her and

given to another. She was demoted from her position as queen.

We don't know why Queen Vashti chose not to submit to her husband. She may have been too busy with her own feast that she was having for the women. She might have felt too modest to appear before so many lustful men. She may have asserted her self-will because she was angry with her drunken husband for making such a request. The Scripture simply does not reveal the motivation for her actions.

This story does, however, raise the question often asked: is there ever a time when we can refuse to submit to those who are in authority over us?

The writer of Hebrews tells us to obey those who rule over us, since they are accountable to God for our souls (Heb. 13:17). Paul tells us to submit to our husbands (Eph. 5:22), and reminds us to pray for all who are in authority that we might lead quiet and peaceful lives (1 Tim. 2:1-2). We know from Psalms 75:6, 7 that promotion comes from the Lord; He raises up authority and He puts it down.

We all like to justify ourselves when we don't want to submit to some particular authority in a particular situation. Women especially tend to have this attitude toward their husbands. Yet God has set a divine order in the home, and He will protect the woman who submits to her husband, regardless of how "spiritual" he is or is not. God will bless us if we have a submissive attitude to all those who are in authority. God works through delegated authority, and we must have the fear of the Lord in us if we choose to disobey the authority God has placed over us.

In the book of Acts, we find an interesting account of Peter and some other apostles, who chose to disobey the priests of the temple by continuing to teach and preach in the name of Jesus. When charged with disobedience, Peter responded that they had to obey God rather than man. Jesus had commanded them to go into all the world to teach and to preach. He had given them authority to do this in His name, and it was by the power in His name that many signs and wonders followed them. They had a choice: to do as Jesus had commanded them, or to obey the priests of the temple, who asked them to not do what Jesus had said.

There may be times in our lives when we must choose to disobey an authority in order to obey God. This is especially true in the day in which we live, for we are told in 1 and 2 Timothy that, in the last days, false teachers will try to deceive us by teaching doctrines which are not of God. Peter gives a whole chapter warning us of false teachers and prophets who give us only partial truth (2 Pet. 2). Even today, many cult leaders brainwash people into submitting to them by replacing God's Word with their own teachings. We need to beware of groups or teachers who have their own revelations beyond God's written word.

How do we know when to submit to man and when to obey God? First, we need to consider the question: Am I being asked to do something against God and His Word? To do this, we need to know the whole counsel of God. It behooves each of us to search the Scriptures, to ask God to show us His truth. The Holy Spirit is that Spirit of truth, and unless He is guiding us, we can easily fall into deception.

Then, as in the case of submission to a particular group or leader, we ought to look for the fruits of a ministry. We are reminded (Matt. 7:15-22) how we are sometimes deceived by the display of the gifts of power. We see many seemingly wonderful works done in the name of Jesus, but the lives of those who minister are full of iniquity. A good tree will bring forth good fruit, and an evil tree will bring forth evil fruit.

We should also be a part of a believing Body where correction can be given. Our fellow Christians may have insight that we do not have. The writer of Hebrews reminds us not to forsake the assembling of ourselves together, but to exhort one another, especialy as we see the day of the Lord approaching (Heb. 10:25).

Most of all, we need to ask the Lord for a liberal amount of wisdom before we take any action, particularly if we think we should not submit to the authority over us. With genuine fear of the Lord, we must act in faith. Faith pleases God. He knows our hearts and He will know if we are rebellious in our attitude toward obedience, or if we truly desire to submit to Him.

Dear Heavenly Father, I thank you for your mercy towards me, that you do love me enough to protect me and guide me. I do ask that your truth would prevail in my life, giving me the wisdom I need every day. I would ask also for the courage to do your will, even when it is very, very hard. Amen.

ESTHER

A WOMAN WHO EXPERIENCED THE POWER RELEASED IN FASTING

Esther 3:8-4:16; 9:1-5; Matt. 6:16-18

Blow the trumpet in Zion, sanctify a fast, call a solemn assembly:

Gather the people, sanctify the congregation, assemble the elders, gather the children, and those that suck the breasts: let the bridegroom go forth of his chamber, and the bride out of her closet.

Let the priests, the ministers of the Lord, weep between the porch and the altar, and let them say, Spare thy people, O Lord, and give not thine heritage to reproach, that the heathen should rule over them: wherefore should say they among the people, Where is their God?

Then will the Lord be jealous for his land, and pity his people.   Joel 2:15-18

The decree had gone out. King Ahasuerus had sent letters to all his provinces, commanding that every Jew—young, old, children, women, men—be put to death on a certain date. It was terrible news for the Jews, who were then exiles in the land of Persia. And it was all because Mordecai, a palace official and a Jew, had refused to bow down to Haman, the king's right-hand man.

What the king did not know was that his beautiful Queen Esther was also a Jew! She was the young virgin chosen to take Queen Vashti's place when she had been dethroned. Furthermore, he did not know that Mordecai was her cousin, that he had raised her after her parents had died and so was a close advisor to her. Queen Esther was, indeed, in a spot—her own husband had commanded that she be put to death!

Esther was deeply grieved when she heard the news. She was sad for her own people, who had already endured many hardships as foreigners in this country. When this decree was made known among them, they wept and wailed and lay in sackcloth and ashes, mourning their fate. She was fearful for Mordecai, since he had been the cause of this decision to annihilate the Jews. She knew that he had had to choose between submitting to an official of the land or remaining true to God. She knew he must feel much sorrow for what would soon happen to his fellow men. As if these concerns were not enough, she couldn't help but wonder what would happen to her. What could she do? Who would understand her situation? How could she save her people?

Through an intermediary, Esther was able to communicate with Mordecai. Mordecai wanted her to go before the king, tell him that she was also a Jew, and ask for deliverance for her people. He told her that perhaps God had raised her up to this position for exactly this purpose. In turn, she reminded him that she could not approach the king unless he called for her, and he had not done that for thirty days.

Faced with an impossible situation, Esther made a most important decision. She asked Mordecai to gather together all the Jews in Shushan for three full days of fasting. She and her maidens would join them. At the end of this time, she would go to the king, praying that God would open the door so she could speak to him. God was her only source of help, and she would humble herself before Him with prayer and fasting.

What can be accomplished by prayer and fasting? We do not know. No human being understands the battles that go on in the heavenlies. We can't imagine the powers and principalities that are overcome just because we deny ourselves food. Fasting for a certain purpose does not always produce a particular result. Nor can we twist God's arm to do our will by praying and fasting.

As with Esther, we have to leave the result of our fast up to God. She fasted by faith, in obedience to Him. As it turned out, she was given favor in the sight of the king and her people were spared. But it didn't come about in the way one might expect. As usual, God worked out the circumstances differently than we would have, and the result was even better than we could have imagined! For, not only did the king issue a counter-decree so that the Jews would be spared, but Mordecai became a hero while Haman went to the gallows!

Why, then, should we fast? We do it because it is God's way of allowing us to participate in His plan and purpose. He wants us to believe, to have faith in Him, to know that He is able when we are not. We find such examples throughout the Bible. Matthew tells us the story of an epileptic boy whom the disciples tried to help. When they couldn't, Jesus ministered to the boy and he was healed. He told the disciples that deliverance comes, in some cases, only by prayer and fasting (Matt. 17:14-21). In Acts (13:1-4), we are told that the early church leaders fasted and prayed, then laid hands on Saul and Barnabas for the work God had called them to do. Jesus fasted himself, as did Moses, David, Daniel, and Paul. Even though the disciples of Jesus did not fast while He was on earth with them, He expected them to return to fasting when He left them.

God chooses fasts for a purpose. Through our fasting, He will bring deliverance, healing, guidance, restoration. Esther did as the prophet Joel admonished us: "Blow the trumpet in Zion, sanctify a fast, call a solemn assembly . . . Then will the Lord be jealous for his land, and pity his people." Deliverance did come for Esther and her people as a result!

Do we have an impossible need in our own lives, one that will take the supernatural intervention of God to be resolved? Do we know of other situations where every human effort has been made to work out a solution? God is bigger than we are. He can fight battles for us. All He asks is that we humble ourselves before Him, pray and fast as we throw ourselves on His mercy. What have we got to lose? Like Esther, we can say, "If I perish, I perish!" Like Esther, too, perhaps we have "come to the kingdom for such a time as this!"

Dear God, I thank you that you are God Almighty, not limited by my human understanding. Give me the faith to trust you, to believe that by my own denial of myself you will somehow do a mighty work of release. I need that release of deliverance, of health, of guidance, of restoration in my own life. Help thou my unbelief, especially when it comes to fasting. Amen.

JOB'S WIFE

A WOMAN WHO LET CIRCUMSTANCES MAKE HER BITTER

Job 1:1-2:10; 42:12-17; Heb. 12:11-15

> For my thoughts are not your thoughts, neither
> are your ways my ways, saith the Lord. For as the
> heavens are higher than the earth, so are my ways
> higher than your ways, and my thoughts than
> your thoughts.   Isa. 55:8, 9

Job had an exceptionally good wife, one who helped him be the perfect and upright man that God said he was. She must have known how to encourage her husband in his business, for we are told that Job was the most wealthy man in his country, with seven thousand sheep, three thousand camels, and hundreds of oxen and cattle. With ten children to raise, Job's wife had many family obligations as well! As women, we know that the responsibilities of a wife and mother are endless, and that many of the most time-consuming jobs of a household go unnoticed.

Job's wife recognized her husband as the true priest of the household. He cared for the spiritual welfare of his seven sons and three daughters. From the little we know of their lives, we can assume that Job's wife was a busy, capable, loving woman—one who was blessed in every way.

Neither Job nor his wife were aware of the battle going on in the heavenlies over Job. They did not know that God would allow Satan to afflict Job so that He could prove that Job was, indeed, a perfect and upright man, and that Job's worship of God was not just the result of his being materially blessed. The Lord let Satan strip Job of all his earthly possessions and eventually his health to reveal Job's heart.

One by one, calamities befell Job and his household. First, a group of marauders stole all his oxen and slew his servants. Next fire fell from heaven and burned up his sheep, while another band of thieves stole all of his camels. As if this was not enough, a great wind blew down the house on top of all his children, killing them. What did Job do? How did he react to all these disasters? He rent his clothes, shaved his head, fell down upon the ground and *worshiped,* saying, "Naked came I out of my mother's womb, and naked shall I return thither: the Lord gave, and the Lord hath taken away; blessed be the name of the Lord." In all that happened, Job did not blame God! He trusted Him in spite of the circumstances. He reacted by praising God. He did as Paul tells us to do: "In every thing give thanks: for this is the will of God in Christ Jesus concerning you" (1 Thess. 5:18).

We have no further comment from Job, even when Satan dealt him one final blow and covered him with boils from head to toe. He merely sat quietly in a pile of ashes and scraped the oozing pus with a piece of broken pottery.

This proved to be the last straw for Job's wife, however. She vented her anger toward both Job and God when she bitterly cried out, "Dost thou still retain thine integrity? Curse God and die!" That was it! There was no way she could praise God for all that had happened to them! When her circumstances changed, so did her trust in the Lord.

A seed of bitterness found root in her heart and she became angry at the whole world and at God in particular. We can see in Job's wife how self-pity then grew out of her bitterness. She viewed everything in relation to herself and her own little world. As with Job's wife, we can easily feel sorry for ourselves, and we affect all those around us as we, too, lash out at God. This is why bitterness is referred to by the writer of Hebrews as a root (Heb. 12:15). It takes hold, grows, and entwines itself around things until it is very difficult to remove. It also feeds and affects everything connected to it.

How do we keep from becoming bitter? We follow the example of Job. We humble ourselves before the Lord in repentance. We forgive those who may have caused our circumstances to change. Then, we thank God. We show Him, by our praise and thanksgiving, that we trust Him. We praise Him for all of our circumstances, good or bad. We praise Him because we trust that He is working all things together for good in our lives, even though we may not see how this can be done. We praise Him because He is worthy, not just because He is blessing us. As we do this, all self-pity, which has been nurtured by a root in bitterness, will wither and die.

As we read the story of Job, we find that he endured all his trials without becoming bitter and in the end was fully restored to the Lord. He passed the test. We remember Job's wife, however, for ten angry words; she let Job down when he needed her love and compassion the most. Though we never again read of Job's wife, we can conclude that somehow during Job's time of testing, she saw her own sin, repented, and learned to praise the Lord as she accepted her circumstances. For when God restored everything to Job, He also gave him seven more sons and three more daughters! The Lord blessed the latter end of Job—and his wife—more than the beginning. We like to think that, in the process, Job's wife learned that it doesn't really pay to let circumstances make one bitter.

Dear God, I want to praise you for who you are, not for what you have given me. Help me put my trust in you and not in the circumstances of life. I do thank you for my husband, for giving him to me for bad times as well as for good, in sickness and in health, in lean times as well as in prosperity. Lord, help me to keep any bitterness from taking root in my life. I do repent of those feelings of resentment and anger. Help me to deal with them as your Holy Spirit shows them to me. Amen.

GOMER

A WOMAN WHO EXPERIENCED GOD'S ENDURING MERCY

Hos. 1:1-2:20; Matt. 9:10-13

And I will sow her unto me in the earth; and I will
have mercy upon her that had not obtained
mercy; and I will say to them which were not my
people, Thou art my people; and they shall say,
Thou art my God.   Hos. 2:23

When God wants His message to be heard, He gives it
through a person who has worked out His Word in his life.
He knows that we are more apt to listen to a person who has
experienced the dealings of the Lord than one who who has
not. We know, for instance, that when Corrie ten Boom said
"Jesus is Victor," she knew what she spoke of from living His
victory many months in the hellish surroundings of a prison
camp during World War II. When we hear Joni Eareckson
Tada testify of God's love and goodness even though she has
lost the use of her arms and legs from an accident, we can be
assured that God will never leave or forsake us, whatever
happens to our bodies.

God so dealt with His servants in Bible times as well. He
took Moses to the far side of the desert where, for forty

years, He trained him to be the shepherd He could trust to lead His people into the Promised Land. The Lord allowed Joseph to be thrown into a pit and a jail, so he would not be overcome with pride when God exalted him as a ruler in order to save His people.

In like fashion, God had a message He wanted to work through His man Hosea. He wanted to speak to His unfaithful people about His love and His mercy. He loved His people very much. In fact, He likened himself to them as a man to his wife. He longed to have a beautiful relationship with His people, but like an unfaithful wife, they forsook Him for other gods.

To illustrate this message, God gave the prophet Hosea a wife named Gomer. She was a prostitute, a woman completely given to sensuality. She was truly a "wife of whoredoms," having had one adulterous relationship after another. To the union of Hosea and Gomer were born three children, each of whom was given a name that described the changing relationship between God and Israel. Through this family, God symbolized His enduring mercy.

Gomer never deserved Hosea's love; she was unfaithful even after she became a mother and had the responsibility of children. Yet Hosea continued to love her in spite of what she did, just as God continues to love us in spite of what we have done.

In His love for us, God does not overlook chastisement when we need it, just as bestowing His mercy upon Israel did not mean that He would not punish them. In fact, discipline is part of mercy. We know that from our relationship with our own children. It is because we truly love them and are merciful to them, that we punish them when they have done wrong. So God judged Israel of their sins.

The attribute of mercy that God wanted to reveal through the example of Hosea and Gomer was "everlastingness." His mercy toward us is new every morning (Lam. 3:22-23). He doesn't turn His mercy on one day and off the next. He is faithful and His mercy endures *forever*.

We don't know if Gomer ever appreciated Hosea's mercy toward her; neither do we always appreciate the mercy of God in our lives. Often, we either don't see it, or we take it for granted.

We don't know how many of God's people heard the lesson God tried to teach through Hosea and Gomer. To those who did hear, He promised a wonderful thing. "I will heal their backsliding, I will love them freely, for mine anger is turned away from him." God would forgive all their unfaithfulness if they would return to Him. He would forget His anger if they would only recognize the fact that they, as a nation, were His wife and He was still their loving husband.

God's mercy toward us is incomprehensible, though we are told many, many times in His word that His mercy endures forever. Forever! That included Gomer in Hosea's time and it includes us living today. As she experienced God's mercy, so also can we.

O give thanks unto the Lord: for he is good:
because his mercy endureth for ever.

Let Israel now say, that His mercy endureth for ever.

Let the house of Aaron now say, that his mercy endureth for ever.

Let them now that fear the Lord say, that his mercy endureth for ever.

Thou art my God, and I will praise thee:
thou art my God, I will exalt thee.

O give thanks unto the Lord; for he is good:
for his mercy endureth for ever.

Ps. 118:1-4, 28, 29

ELISABETH

THE FIRST WOMAN TO RECOGNIZE JESUS AS HER LORD
Luke 1:5-45; Dan. 7:13, 14

> Howbeit when he, the Spirit of truth, is come, he
> will guide you into all truth: for he shall not speak
> of himself; but whatsoever he shall hear, that shall
> he speak: and he will show you things to come. He
> shall glorify me: for he shall receive of mine, and
> shall shew it unto you.   John 16:13, 14

It must have been quite a meeting between Mary and
Elisabeth. The two cousins, a young girl and an older
woman, had something quite unusual in common. They
were both to be very special mothers, though neither one
should have been expecting a baby.

Elisabeth, wife of the priest Zacharias, was past
the childbearing age. A few months earlier, the angel
Gabriel had announced to her husband that she would have
a son whom they would name John. Mary, on the other
hand, was a young virgin betrothed to a man named Joseph.
Gabriel had appeared to her personally and informed her
that she would conceive by the Holy Spirit and bear a son
who would be called Jesus. These two women became

mothers because of God's supernatural intervention in their lives!

Mary and Elisabeth probably had much to talk about during the three months that they spent together, especially since Elisabeth's husband couldn't speak at all! They probably reviewed again and again the visits of the angel Gabriel. They ignored the inevitable gossip about their condition. They wondered why God was sending special sons for them to raise.

However, it was the first conversation between the two pregnant women that was so significant. When Elisabeth first heard Mary at the door, the babe leaped in her womb, and she was filled with the Holy Ghost (Luke 1:41). Her first words to Mary recognized her cousin as the mother of her *Lord.* Mary responded that her spirit rejoiced in God, her Savior.

We all need to recognize in our own lives the two titles of Jesus that are revealed here: Jesus as Savior and Jesus as Lord. Many people confess Jesus as Savior, and call upon Him to save them out of all situations in this life. But not all acknowledge Jesus as their *Lord.* This requires a deeper commitment. It means that we are willing to follow and obey Him in everything, to totally commit our lives to Him, to deny our flesh, because we are crucified with Him.

To understand the lordship of Jesus in our lives, we must see the relationship between a master and his servant. A master purchases a servant because he has something for him to do. Jesus purchased us with His blood at Calvary. Though we accept this work of atonement for our sins by His grace, He has a work for us to do, if we choose to recognize Him as our master.

A master expects his servant to obey him. Jesus expects us to do His work, to obey His commands, to live our lives as He directs. A master feels especially honored and blessed when his servant obeys him out of love for the master and not just out of duty. Jesus is blessed and honored as Lord when we do His will because we want to, not because we have to.

No one can say that Jesus is Lord except through the Holy Spirit (1 Cor. 12:3). When we accept Jesus as our Savior, the Holy Spirit lifts Him up so that we begin to see Him as Lord. The more we learn to submit to Jesus as our master—our Lord—the more we understand that master/servant relationship.

Someday, "every knee should bow . . . and every tongue shall confess that Jesus Christ is Lord" (Phil. 2:10, 11). This does not mean that He will necessarily be recognized as Lord personally during the lifetime of each person on earth. "Behold, he cometh with clouds; and every eye shall see him, and they also which pierced him: and all kindreds of the earth shall wail [or mourn] because of him (Rev. 1:7). Some will recognize Him as Lord of all creation and regret that they didn't acknowledge Him as their personal Lord (as well as Savior) earlier.

Elisabeth, by the power of the Holy Spirit, recognized Jesus as her Lord, even *before* His birth. How much more do we, who live after His life, death and resurrection have the opportunity to see Jesus in this light? We know that in His death He demonstrated victory over Satan. He triumphed over the last enemy, death, as He rose from the tomb. We can know, by the power of the Holy Spirit in our lives, that He is indeed Lord of all creation and that He is worthy of our allegiance. Jesus is Lord of Lords! Will we, as did Elisabeth, recognize Him as "my Lord?"

Dear Jesus, I am so grateful for your saving power and that you care what happens to me, both now and in eternity. But, dear Jesus, help me also to see you as Lord of my life, as the master who requires my total allegiance as a servant. You alone are worthy. Amen.

MARY, MOTHER OF JESUS

A WOMAN WHO HAD MUCH TO PONDER IN HER HEART

Luke 1:26-38; 2:8-35, 42-48; John 19:25-27

And Simeon blessed them, and said unto Mary his mother, Behold, this child is set for the fall and rising again of many in Israel; and for a sign which shall be spoken against; (Yea a sword shall pierce through thy own soul also,) that the thoughts of many hearts may be revealed.   Luke 2:34, 35

Mary, the mother of Jesus, is probably the most recognized woman of the Bible; yet, she is probably the least known as a person. Many things happened in her life, but we are not told how she felt, or what she thought. Let's look at some of these incidents:

The angel Gabriel appeared to her, an unmarried young woman, and told her that through supernatural means she would conceive a child who would be called the Son of the Highest, who would reign over the house of Jacob forever, and whose kingdom would have no end. What did Mary say in response to this announcement? "Be it unto me according to thy word."

When this child was born, the shepherds on the nearby

hills of Bethlehem came to His birthplace, the stable, and told Mary and Joseph that the angels had announced His birth to them. What did Mary do? She "kept all these things, and pondered them in her heart."

When Mary and Joseph took Jesus to the temple for presentation to the Lord, Simeon recognized the baby as the Lord's Christ, and prophesied over Jesus. As this happened, Joseph and Mary "marvelled at those things which were spoken of him."

When Jesus was twelve years old, Mary and Joseph took him to the temple in Jerusalem, where He talked with the learned men, and He told His parents that He must be about His Father's business. When they returned to Nazareth, Mary "kept all these sayings in her heart."

Think of the things Mary must have pondered in her heart! "What does it mean that I will conceive by the Holy Ghost and bear God's only Son? How will I raise Him, especially since I am not yet married? Why was I chosen to be this Child's mother? Why did God announce His birth to some shepherds and not to more prominent people? How did the angels appear in the sky? What did Simeon mean when he said that Jesus would be 'a light to lighten the Gentiles, and the glory of thy people Israel'? What is 'His Father's business,' anyway? On and on we could go, thinking of questions we would have in our minds and hearts if some of these events had happened to us!

Yet, each of us has things that occur in our lives which we don't understand. We have trials and problems which seem to have no solution. We are put in places that we did not choose. On the other hand, we see little miracles that are meaningful only to ourselves, and, sometimes, we have insights that only we understand. We too have much to ponder in our hearts.

Sometimes God just wants us to himself, to think on His ways, His love, His glory. He created us for His pleasure (Rev. 4:11); therefore, He wants us to talk things over with Him and to enjoy Him. Some things are meant to be just between ourselves and our Father in heaven.

When Jesus was just a baby being presented to the Lord in the temple, Simeon gave Mary a prophecy which she probably also pondered in her heart many times, wondering what it meant. He told her that the thoughts of many hearts would be revealed through her child and that a sword would pierce her own soul. This prophecy was fulfilled when Jesus died.

Imagine the things Mary must have suffered as she watched Jesus increasingly given to His Father's business while being tried and ridiculed. Imagine her agony, as she watched her first-born son, stripped, beaten, and then nailed to a cross, where she watched Him hang until He died.

We all have questions concerning life and death, especially in the area of suffering, asking "why" about things we don't understand. God didn't reveal all the answers even to the very one He choose to be the mother of His Son. If Mary had wanted to ask questions of God, we certainly would understand. Yet she didn't ask one "why." She accepted God's way.

What was the outcome of Mary's pondering of things in her heart and her refusal to question God? She was specifically named in the list of those present when the Holy Spirit was given in power at Pentecost (Acts 1:13-14; 2:1-4). She was among the first to receive the Holy Spirit in all its fullness. She was given the Comforter and the Spirit of Truth. Many of the answers to things she had pondered in her heart were now revealed to her, and she was comforted.

Let us not be afraid to wait for answers to questions that seem to have no answer. Let us look to the Holy Spirit, as we invite Him into our lives, to reveal the truth and to comfort us. Let us enjoy sweet communion with God, as He so ordained. Like Mary, let us accept those things which happen to us and ponder them with Him in our hearts.

Dear Heavenly Father, teach me to meditate on your Word and to ponder in my heart the truths you have for me. Help me also to be content with your timing in revealing answers. Bless all those who lead lonely lives, because no other human being understands their suffering. You do, and I thank you for the comfort you give. Amen.

ANNA

A WOMAN WHO WAS REWARDED FOR HER FAITHFULNESS IN PRAYER

Luke 2:36-38; Rom. 8:26, 27, 34

> Watch ye therefore, and pray always, that ye may
> be accounted worthy to escape all these things
> that shall come to pass, and to stand before the
> Son of man.   Luke 21:36

Picture Anna, a little old woman, who served the Lord in the temple with continual prayer and fasting. It may not seem unusual at first, but when we read the three verses of Scripture that tell us of her, we learn some interesting facts. She was a prophetess; God had not spoken through the prophets for hundreds of years. She was of the tribe of Asher, not the tribe usually associated with the temple worship. She was an eighty-four-year-old widow, definitely past the prime of life. In our natural minds, we would say that Anna was a poor candidate for any job, let alone for a vital ministry needed by the Lord to carry out His plan for mankind!

Sometimes we think that, because God has said He will do something, all we have to do is just sit back and wait. We don't know that we have a part in making His will come to pass. We don't understand what He wants and expects us to do. We don't realize the tremendous privilege and responsibility we have in the ministry of prayer and intercession. Yet this is one of the mysterious ways God has of accomplishing His will.

God could have saved His chosen people from the many years of wandering in the wilderness, but He chose to let Moses intercede for them, to plead His mercy on their behalf. God could have delivered the Israelites from the Babylonian captivity supernaturally, but He let Daniel, as he stood in the king's palace, fast and pray for the people. Ezra interceded for the Jews, after they returned from exile. God always raises up intercessors to "pray in" His will.

When, four hundred years after the time of the prophets, God sent His only begotten Son into the world to become the atonement for sin, He looked down upon earth and found a little old lady, giving herself continually to prayers and fastings, day and night. He saw her work of intercession, which pleased Him. He must have revealed to her that He was sending the Redeemer of Israel in the form of a baby, for when Joseph and Mary later brought the baby Jesus into the temple for presentation unto the Lord, she recognized instantly who He was.

What a reward for her faithfulness! God allowed her to see the baby Jesus and to recognize Him as the Redeemer sent by God. Her prayers had been answered.

God needs intercessors today. He needs Annas willing to continually fast and pray, claiming His Word that His kingdom truly come upon earth as it is in Heaven. He needs those who will help pray His Word and His will into being. How can we do this?

As sons of God, we have the privilege of coming boldly before the throne of God because of the blood of Jesus (Heb. 4:16, 10:19). Just as the death of Christ brought Him into a place of intercession for us (Rom. 8:34), so our death with Him to sin and self sets us free to intercede for others. As we abide in Him, and His words abide in us, we desire that His will be done in not only our own lives, but also in the lives of others. So we pray, bringing people, needs, and situations before God. God then uses this intercession to save souls, change circumstances, extend His mercy—essentially, to perform His Word on earth. To help us do this, God has made His Holy Spirit available to us so that we can know how to pray as we ought. This Spirit within us knows God's will and makes intercession for us with groanings which cannot be uttered (Rom. 8:26, 27).

We have much to pray for as we see the enemy coming like a flood into our world, our country, our homes, our schools, our churches, and yes, into our very own families (Isa. 59:19). Every day, many needs come to our attention, and He wants us to lift these needs up to Him so that He can fulfill His Word.

As Anna was faithful, she was blessed to see Jesus at His first coming. How exciting it is to us today to know that, as we watch and pray, we can have a part in His second coming! We, too, will be rewarded in seeing the Lord's Christ! Hallelujah!

Dear Jesus, I thank you not only for dying for me and for the resurrection which assures me of the new life, but I especially thank you for being there at the right hand of God interceding for me today. Because you are that great high priest, I can come boldly into the throne of grace and find help in a time of need. Help me, too, to intercede for others' needs, as they come to my attention today. I look forward to your coming to earth again! Amen.

HERODIAS

A WOMAN WHO TOOK REVENGE

Mark 6:4-6, 14-29; Ps. 94:1-11; Rom. 2:1-16

Rejoice, O ye nations, with his people: for he will avenge the blood of his servants, and will render vengeance to his adversaries, and will be merciful unto his land, and to his people.   Deut. 32:43

John the Baptist came into our world for a special purpose—to prepare the way for Jesus. He came to call people to repentance, to help them see themselves as sinners in need of a Savior. Malachi, the last prophet of the Old Testament, said that before the Lord came, Elijah would come first to turn the hearts of the fathers to the children, and the hearts of the children to their fathers (Mal. 4:5, 6). Jesus said that John the Baptist fulfilled this prophecy (Matt. 11:13-15). John had come to call people into right relationship with one another and with God.

We all know that John the Baptist preached to great crowds in the wilderness, but evidently he also spoke with individuals as well. He specifically told Herod the Tetrarch that it was wrong for him to live with Herodias, his brother's wife (Mark 6:18).

This made Herod so angry that he had John put in prison. It made Herodias angry too, and she sought to get even. She

161

used Herod's birthday party for an occasion to exact revenge. Her daughter's dancing before Herod pleased the tetrarch so much that he did a foolish thing. He swore that he would give her whatever she desired, which she decided, after consultation with her mother, was the head of John the Baptist. Herod was aghast, but he couldn't refuse her request in front of all the people who had heard him make the offer. He gave the order, and John's head was brought upon a platter for all to see. Herodias had taken vengeance into her own hands.

What do we do when we are told truth about ourselves and don't want to face it? Our first reaction is usually to justify ourselves and blame someone or something else. It's hard to accept criticism, even when it is designed to help us. We don't like to face sin in ourselves. As Herodias' refusal to see her own sin led her into committing another one (murder), so we are in danger of the same thing. When we refuse to look at the fault which has been pointed out in us, we tend to take revenge in some way.

We are told in the Word that vengeance belongs to God alone. God is the judge. God's judgment includes qualities that ours does not. First, God's judgment is "according to truth" (Rom. 2:2). He is not biased as we are; He sees the whole picture.

Second, His judgment is "according to deeds" (Rom. 2:6) and "according to works" (Rev. 20:12). He knows all of man's works, those which are as gold, silver and precious stone, and those which are only hay, wood, and stubble (1 Cor. 3:12-15).

Third, we find that God is no respecter of persons (Rom. 2:11). We are very prejudiced persons. We take criticism from the people we like but not from those we don't like. God, in His merciful love, is more objective. He judges a person according to the way he's acted, with the insight and knowledge he has received.

Finally, Paul says that God will judge the secrets of men by Jesus Christ "according to my gospel" (Rom. 2:16). In other words, our relationship with Jesus will affect the judgment upon us.

God's judgment was upon Herodias, because she would not accept the accusation of John the Baptist pointing out her sin. She did not gratefully accept the rebuke so that she could get right with God. She was not willing to let God judge her, so that, in His mercy, He could bring her to himself. She chose rather to get rid of the accuser, John the Baptist. She thought that she would solve everything by taking vengeance into her own hands. She did not judge according to truth and according to works, as does God.

Herodias had not learned to face criticism, to look at her own heart, and to let God judge her. She usurped God's position of judge and put a man to death.

Imagine the reaction of both Herod and Herodias when they heard of the fame of Jesus, and thought He was John the Baptist risen from the dead!

What was the end of Herodias, the Jezebel of the New Testament? According to the historian Josephus, she was the ruin of Herod. She tried to get him to demand the title of king. Agrippa saw to it that this demand was refused, and Herod was banished and ended his days in shame and exile. Herodias was proud; she remained faithful to her husband in the disgrace that she herself caused.

Dear God, I thank you for the people you send into my life to point out my sin, for they can help me face those things which hurt my relationship with you. I especially thank you for sending Jesus that my sins can be forgiven. Help me, Lord, to leave all judgment to you, no matter how much I may feel like "getting even." I trust you and your love for me. Amen.

THE WOMAN OF SAMARIA

A WOMAN WHO FOUND SATISFACTION FOR HER THIRST

John 4:5-30; John 6:35; Rev. 22:17

> Blessed are they which do hunger and thirst after
> righteousness: for they shall be filled. Matt. 5:6

The Samaritan woman picked up her waterpot and
headed for the town well. It was noontime, and most of the
women of Sychar had already drawn their daily supply of
water from Jacob's well. But this woman wanted to go at a
time when she would not likely be seen, at a time when the
other women would be at home preparing a meal. She was
afraid of talk and gossip: they knew she was living with a
man to whom she was not married, after having five
husbands. She felt their judgment upon her and purposely
chose to go to the well alone.

When she arrived at the well, however, she was surprised
to see a man sitting there, obviously weary from his journey.
She was even more surprised to note that He was a Jew,
because the Jews did not usually come through Samaria.
When this Jew, Jesus, asked her for a drink, she questioned
His presence there and why He would ask her, a Samaritan,
to give Him a drink of water. Jesus told her that if she knew

who He was, she would ask for living water and not for this water which could not keep her from becoming thirsty again. This living water appealed to her, for she wanted her spiritual thirst quenched, plus a source of water that meant she would not have to come to the well any more.

As Jesus continued to speak, she perceived that He was a prophet, and began to converse with Him in earnest. She had found one who had the answers to her questions. She knew that the Messiah would come someday and tell them all things; she had been awaiting His arrival. Perhaps her messed-up life had helped her realize that she needed a Savior. She thirsted, and Jesus, who could cleanse her from sin and restore her to a right relationship with himself, satisfied this thirst.

After she was convinced that He could, indeed, be the Christ, she left her waterpot and ran into the city, shouting to all the men to come and see the man at the well. Many responded, heard Jesus' message also, and believed on Him.

Later that year, at the Feast of Tabernacles, Jesus urged people to come and drink of Him, if they thirsted. He added that he who believed on Him would have rivers of living water flow from his belly (John 7:37, 38). As we drink of Jesus, He, the Living Water, will not only satisfy our deepest thirst, but will then flow from us to reveal himself to others. Those who have come to Jesus for immersion in the Holy Spirit know a quenching of their thirst for God that can't be obtained any other way.

It is sad to see people around us who do not appear thirsty for spiritual nourishment, who outwardly are satisfied with life and see no need of anything different. They have been caught up in the ways of the world to satisfy their lust, whether it be obtaining possessions, seeking pleasure, or climbing the ladder of success. Maybe, like the Samaritan woman at the well, their lives will have to be messed up before they will recognize their need for a drink of Living Water.

What then is our role as believers, as ones who know the source of that Living Water? We are salt! (Matt. 5:13.) We are that ingredient which God uses to help make others thirsty. By ourselves, as Christians, we can't benefit others; but, when we get mixed up with non-believers, we can become a seasoning and create a thirst. The more of Jesus that people see in us, whether they know Him or not, the more thirsty they become. They begin to see that He is the only one that will truly satisfy.

He is that Living Water of which He told the Woman of Samaria. He satisfied her thirst, as He has for everyone since then who has drunk of Him.

Dear God, Thank you for putting those salty people in my life, who helped me to thirst for more of you. Thank you, too, for Jesus, who filled me with the Living Water. Help me to be that salt which will help make others thirsty until they, too, immerse themselves in your Spirit and find Jesus, who can satisfy every need they have. And,

> *"Fill my cup, Lord, I lift it up, Lord,*
> *Come and quench this thirsting of my soul,*
> *Bread of heaven, feed me till I want no more.*
> *Fill my cup, fill it up and make me whole."*
> > *Amen.*

Fill My Cup, Lord by Richard Blanchard
Copyright 1959, assigned to Sacred Songs 1964.
Copyright 1971 by Word, Inc.

THE WIDOW OF NAIN

A WOMAN WHOSE WEEPING BROUGHT FORTH MINISTRY FROM JESUS

Luke 7:11-17; Ps. 30:1-12

Blessed are ye that weep now: for ye shall laugh.
Luke 6:21b

Jesus understands the range of human emotions. He was the Word made flesh; He can identify with us, for He lived on earth as a man. True, He was more than a man, He was God incarnate; but Scripture reminds us that He was a Man of Sorrows and acquainted with grief (Isa. 53:3). John tells us that Jesus himself wept when He was with His bereaved friends, Mary and Martha, even though He knew that the miracle soon to take place would bring them utter joy (John 11:35). Jesus knows us, and He has compassion on us.

The widow of Nain was crying when Jesus saw her. Her only son had died, and his body was being carried to the tomb for burial. Perhaps her sorrow reminded her of her husband's death and of the loneliness that now lay ahead. She wondered who would care for her now, and how she would live. She wasn't crying out to Jesus; she probably wasn't even aware that He was around.

Jesus and His followers had just entered the city. In the midst of the crowds of people, He heard her muffled sobbing. He saw her weeping, and He was moved with compassion. He then performed the first miracle of raising the dead since the time of the prophets. It was a sign to the people that He was sent of God. "Young man," He said, "I say to thee, Arise!" The man immediately sat up and began to speak. Jesus gave him back to his mother, and the crowd proclaimed, "God hath visited his people." The widow of Nain's tears of grief turned to tears of joy.

There are many kinds of tears, even tears of happiness and gratefulness. We all have experienced tears of self-pity, anger, frustration and depression. At some time during our lives, we have shed tears of grief over the loss of a loved one, as this widow did. And Jesus knows of all these tears; He died for every one of them.

In a very comforting Scripture, Isaiah describes how God will take back His beloved Israel, though she had much sorrow. "For the Lord hath called thee as a woman forsaken and grieved in spirit, and a wife of youth, when thou was refused, saith thy God. For a small moment have I forsaken thee; but with great mercies will I gather thee. In a little wrath I hid my face from thee for a moment; but with everlasting kindness will I have mercy on thee, saith the Lord thy Redeemer" (Isa. 54:6-8).

When we weep it is difficult to see how the Lord can turn our sorrow into joy, for at that time, we usually feel rejected by God. He can minister to us, if we will only let Him. The widow of Nain didn't cry out to Jesus; she probably wouldn't have expected Him to notice her in the crowd, even if she had known who He was.

Jesus came to her and she let Him minister words of comfort to her aching soul. She let Him come close enough to whisper in her ear, "Weep not." As God would turn grieving Israel back to himself, so Jesus took the initiative in ministering to the widow of Nain.

David was another person who knew what it was to mourn and weep. He also knew that God was the only one who could turn his sorrow into joy, something he himself could not do. He said: "Thou hast turned for me my mourning into dancing: thou hast put off my sackcloth, and girded me with gladness" (Ps. 30:11).

We learn more about sorrow in this Psalm. Sorrow can be brief in duration, although it may seem as if it will last forever. "Weeping may endure for a night, but joy cometh in the morning" (verse 5). In the Sermon on the Mount, Jesus said that those who mourn shall be comforted (Matt. 5:4). There *will* be an end to our tears. Someday God will completely wipe away all tears from our eyes (Rev. 7:17).

Why did God turn David's tears into praise and his mourning into dancing? "To the end that my glory may sing praise to thee!" (Ps. 30:12). God wants our praise. He wants to be glorified. He wants to minister to us when we weep, for He wants us to be filled with joy, that His glory may be revealed.

Let us, during our times of weeping, remember the widow of Nain. Let us allow Jesus to see us and minister to us, as He did to her. He understands and He cares. Let Him wipe away our tears that His glory may be revealed.

Dear Heavenly Father, thank you for understanding me. Thank you, too, for coming to me when I am hurt, so hurt that I don't even want to cry out to you. Your love amazes me and I am humbled by it. Thank you for this love, and that for my tears you died. Amen.

MARY MAGDALENE

A WOMAN WHO HAD A PERSONAL
RELATIONSHIP WITH JESUS

John 20:1-29; Ps. 139

> Behold, what manner of love the Father hath
> bestowed upon us, that we should be called the
> sons of God.   1 John 3:12

What a contrast in the life of Mary Magdalene! She is
mentioned on at least nine different occasions in the
Gospels, both as a woman from whom Jesus cast out seven
demons, as well as the first one to talk with Him following
His resurrection. Jesus made the difference.

When He first met her, demons completely possessed her
body and mind (assuming that the number seven signifies
completion). Since Jesus came to destroy the works of the
devil, He had power over the enemy. He set her free from
total bondage.

This was the beginning of Mary Magdalene's personal
relationship with Jesus. After she allowed Him to come into
her life and cleanse her from all sin, she chose to devote the
rest of her life to Him. She joined the women who followed
Him during His ministry, and was present when He hung
upon the cross. She shared many things with Him, and He

taught her the way of the Kingdom. She believed in Him and she followed Him, because she was grateful for what He had done in her life. And, she allowed Him to communicate with her.

It's interesting to note that her personal relationship with Jesus continued, even after everyone else had given up. She even shared with Him a moment in history that no one else can claim. She had the unique privilege of talking with Jesus between His descent into the lower parts of the earth and His ascent to the Father in Heaven (John 20:17; Eph. 4:9, 10). Mary Magdalene had come to the tomb on the first day of the week following Jesus' crucifixion and burial. She still expected a miracle, though everyone else had given up hope of Jesus being raised from the dead. She knew that Jesus had had power over the enemy in her life; perhaps this knowledge gave her faith to believe that He would also have victory over the last enemy, death. Her perseverance was rewarded when she saw the risen Jesus and recognized Him as her Master.

After she recognized Him, He said, "Touch me not; for I am not yet ascended to my Father." Eight days later, Jesus said to Thomas, "Reach hither thy finger!" He wanted Thomas to touch Him. He had now already ascended to the Father to offer His blood, so He could be touched. Thomas needed the proof, and Jesus understood that. Mary Magdalene did not need to touch Jesus to recognize Him; but Thomas, even though he had walked with the Master for three years, still needed assurance of who Jesus was.

God knows each of our needs, our abilities, our desires. He knows the number of hairs on our heads (Matt. 10:30). David tells us that He has known each of us from our mother's wombs (Ps. 139). It's impossible for us to comprehend how the omnipotent God of the universe can know each one of us so well and be concerned about each one of us personally; but He does, praise God!

At the same time, God wants us to know Him, to have fellowship with Him. He made us in His image, and He wants us to become like Him, to know His nature and to grow in it. We do this by relating to Him, by sharing ourselves with Him in prayer and by reading His Word that it may become a part of us.

In no religion save Christianity can a human being have a personal relationship with his God. This is because no other god sent part of himself, an only begotten Son, into the world to die for the sins of each person. God has shared His own person with us; He wants us to share ourselves with Him. This is the personal relationship that Mary Magdalene had with Jesus, and one that each of us can have as well.

Dear God, I thank you for knowing me as a person, and not just as a number in your whole creation. I am humbled when I realize that you love me so much that you would have sent Jesus to die just for me had I been the only person on earth. Have mercy upon me, O God, as I try to return some of this love to you. Amen.

JOANNA

A WOMAN WHO FREELY
RECEIVED AND THEN FREELY GAVE
Luke 8:1-3, 24:1-10; Eph. 2:8-10

Freely ye have received, freely give. Matt. 10:8b

Joanna was the recipient of God's abundant mercy. She is specifically listed as one of the women who received healing and deliverance from Jesus (Luke 8:1-3). She then became one of the traveling "Marthas," giving of her own substance to serve Jesus in His ministry to others. Perhaps these women cooked the meals and washed the clothes for Jesus and His disciples as they journeyed from place to place. It was truly a life of service, born out of gratefulness for what Jesus had done in their own lives. This group of women were faithful to the end, being present at His crucifixion, and caring for His body during burial rites. They were the first to behold the resurrection and to have the privilege of sharing this exciting news with the disciples.

Joanna's husband is named in Luke: he was Chuza, Herod's steward. He must have been a man of intelligence and ability to have been given the responsibility of handling Herod's business.

One wonders how much opportunity Joanna had to share the good news with other servants of Herod's palace. Did they ask where she had been when she returned from one of her trips? Did they question her about Jesus and what He was saying to the people? Did she tell them of the miracles she had seen, or of the many Gentiles who also followed Him?

Today, God has witnesses in the form of janitors, gardeners, and maids in the households of executives. He has His followers strategically placed in the homes of the rulers of the nations. No person is unimportant in God's total plan of salvation. He especially wants to have those in authority trust Him, for they influence the masses for good or for evil.

There must have been some talk of Jesus and His ministry in the palace, and it had an effect on Herod's family too. There is an interesting phrase in Acts which lists the names of the leaders in the church of Antioch. One of these was, "Manaen, which had been brought up with Herod, the tetrarch" (Acts 13:1). The Open Bible says, in a footnote, that he was Herod's foster brother. Did he believe in Jesus as a result of Joanna's testimony in Herod's household?

Why would Joanna have felt it important to share Jesus with others? She had had a personal experience with Jesus! He had healed her, and she knew it! She had freely received of His grace and mercy. She had received of Him that free gift of God which is eternal life.

Hundreds of years before Joanna lived, God said, "I will heal their backsliding, I will love them freely" (Hos. 14:4). It cost God a great price to give us salvation. Yet, that is how much He loves us. His love is free to us.

Joanna knew that love. She was not content to receive blessings for herself, but she desired to pass this love on. She was not like the Dead Sea, dying because it only receives the Jordan River and has no outlet. She was like the Sea of

Galilee (where Jesus' ministry took place) which both receives the Jordan and sends it out as well. The love of Jesus flowed into her; it flowed out in love and service to Him. Freely she had received; freely she gave.

Dear God, thank you for your free gift of salvation to me. Make me a channel of your love today. Show me someone to whom I can freely give your love, your compassion and your mercy in your name. I love you. Amen.

THE WOMAN WITH
AN ISSUE OF BLOOD

A WOMAN WHO WAS TOUCHED
BY THE LORD WHEN SHE REACHED
OUT TO HIM IN FAITH

Mark 5:25-34; Matt. 4:23, 24

> But without faith it is impossible to please him:
> for he that cometh to God must believe that he is,
> and that he is a rewarder of them that diligently
> seek him. Heb. 11:6

This woman was discouraged. For twelve years she
had been hemorrhaging blood. Though she had gone to
doctor after doctor, she had found no relief. The continual
loss of blood left her very weak—so weak that to leave
the house was a real effort. To add to her discouragement,
she had no money, having used it all trying to regain
her health. As if her mental depression and physical
weakness were not enough, she was an outcast from society.
Her blood condition rendered her ceremonially unclean;
no one wanted to be around her, for whoever touched her
would also be unclean (Lev. 15:25-27). She had no hope
of getting well, no hope of being accepted as a normal
person.

Jesus had come to the area surrounding the Sea of Galilee to teach, to heal, and to minister to the people. On the other side of the sea where He had just been, he had delivered a man from unclean spirits. The news had spread and the crowds now thronged to see Him. Everyone was excited. They all wanted to have a look at the one who had performed so many miracles.

Jairus, one of the rulers of the synagogue, ran to meet Him before He could even get off the boat. His daughter was dying and he wanted Jesus to come lay hands on her that she might be healed.

As the crowd gathered on the seashore, the woman slipped in unnoticed. Because of the excitement, no one saw her resolutely inch her way toward Jesus. "If I may touch but his clothes, I shall be whole," she said to herself (Mark 5:28). She knew Jesus held the answer.

And when her hand touched the hem of Jesus' garment, she knew instantly that she had been healed. At the same time, Jesus felt the healing virtue leave His body. He turned around and asked those near Him who had touched Him.

It would have been easy for the woman to remain silent. If she admitted touching Him, she would be noticed by those around her. Perhaps they would cry out "Unclean!" and all would turn away from her, even Jesus. Instead, in fear and trembling, she fell down at Jesus' feet and confessed that she had been the one to touch His garment. She humbled herself before Him, willing to take the rejection of the crowd, willing to expose herself as she reached to Jesus in faith.

This pleased Jesus. He appreciated her faith and He told her that this very faith in Him made her whole! She was completely healed because she had been willing to reach out to Him, regardless of what others might say or do.

It is easy to imagine this woman finding it safer to have stayed at home. Then she would have had no crowds and no disappointment to face if she were not healed. But she chose to step out in faith and put herself in a position to receive a miracle.

Here's an enlightening exercise: underline all the verses where Jesus healed someone. You will find that He healed all those who came to Him. Even when great multitudes followed Him, "he healed them all" (Matt. 12:15). Mark adds, "and as many as touched him were made whole" (Mark 6:56).

It's interesting to note that the story of the woman with the issue of blood appears in three of the four gospels. It contains a lesson God wants us to learn. He wants us to know that as many as touch Him are made whole!

How can we touch God? How can we reach out and actually come into contact with the hem of His garment? Like the woman in this story, we do it by faith. We believe God, we trust His Word, and we act upon that Word as if it has already happened to us. We must believe that He is, and that He will reward those who diligently seek Him (Heb. 11:6). We must take those steps which will bring us close to Him, such as praying, reading His Word and finding fellowship in His Body. We must want Him more than we want the approval of those around us. As we act in faith, He will reward us, for then He is truly pleased.

Dear Heavenly Father, I look to you, the author and finisher of my faith, to show me how to reach out to you in faith. Give me the courage to believe and to act when I don't see evidence of the answer. I want to please you. Amen.

THE SYRO-PHOENICIAN WOMAN

A WOMAN WHO PERSISTED
UNTIL SHE WAS BLESSED

Matt. 15:21-28; Gen. 32:24-29; Mark 7:24-30

> And he said, Let me go, for the day breaketh.
> And he [Jacob] said, I will not let thee go, except
> thou bless me.   Gen. 32:26

We all remember the story of Jacob and of his wrestle with
an angel the night before he confronted his estranged
brother, Esau. As they wrestled, Jacob refused to let the
angel go until the angel blessed him. Upon receiving this
blessing, Jacob responded by proclaiming that he had seen
God face to face. His persistence had won a blessing for him.

And so it was for the Gentile woman of the coasts of Tyre
and Sidon, who persisted in asking healing from Jesus for
her daughter. This woman was not a Jew; she was not one of
the lost sheep of Israel that Jesus had been sent to save. She
had no right to claim any of God's promises to His people,
but she saw in Jesus something that she needed, and she was
willing to take whatever leftover blessing He could offer.

Jesus did not respond to her cry for help in His usual
compassionate manner. Instead, He seemed to try to
discourage her. The first time she asked for mercy, Jesus

didn't even answer. The second time, He told her that He had not come to the Gentiles, implying that she had no right to ask help from Him. Again, when she humbled herself to worship Him, He referred to her kind as dogs. She was ignored, rejected, and rebuked, and yet she persisted in her plea. She was a mother willing to sacrifice her all, even her reputation, for her daughter's healing.

We don't know why Jesus kept her waiting for the answer; perhaps He was testing her. Through the ages, God has tested people to see what was in their hearts, to see how sincere they really were and how willing they were to persist in what they believed. He did this with His own children, Israel.

Moses told the tribes, "And thou shalt remember all the way which the Lord thy God led thee these forty years in the wilderness, to humble thee, and to prove thee, to know what was in thine heart, whether thou wouldest keep his commandments, or no" (Deut. 8:2). God kept them for a time from entering into the Promised Land, to test their faith in Him, to see what was in their hearts.

Luke gives us a parable told by Jesus to encourage us to pray always and not faint—to persist in prayer. He gives the example of a widow who came to a judge for justice (Luke 18:1-8). The judge put her off several times, but because she kept coming to him to have the matter settled, he finally took her case. Jesus ended the parable by saying, "And shall not God avenge his own elect, which cry day and night unto him, though he bear long with them?" God has more compassion than an unjust judge!

Jesus himself persisted in prayer. On the night before His arrest and trial, He prayed to the Father three times in the Garden of Gethsemane, saying "the same words" (Matt. 26:44).

The Syro-Phoenician woman persisted until she was given

her request. She withstood the testing, even in the face of rejection. She continued asking Jesus for her daughter's healing until He blessed her with the answer.

There are times when we pray once, commit our problems to the Lord, and thank Him for the answer. We know, by faith, that He has heard and He will give us our request.

There are other times, however, when we, too, need to persist in prayer, to "pray through" until the answer comes. Sometimes, we need to humble ourselves and accept God's perfect timing in answering our pleas. Perhaps He is testing our motivation; perhaps He is trying our faith. We are, however, assured that if we ask we will receive, if we seek we will find, and if we knock and keep on knocking the way will be opened unto us (Matt. 7:7).

If Jesus answered the prayer of the Syro-Phoenician woman, who was not one of His chosen people, how much more does He want to answer the prayers of those who are His own children!

Dear God, teach me how to pray. Amen.

MARY OF BETHANY

A WOMAN WHO EXPERIENCED MUCH AT THE FEET OF JESUS

Luke 10:38-42; John 11:1-5, 28-36; 12:1-11; Mark 14:3-9

> Humble yourselves therefore under the mighty
> hand of God, that he may exalt you in due
> time.   1 Pet. 5:6

We in the twentieth century have little to do with the feet of another person, either in a practical or in a figurative way. We never fall at another's feet in adoration. We seldom speak of sitting at anyone's feet to learn, and we don't kiss another's feet and wipe them with our tears and hair! Yet Mary did all three to Jesus! She loved Him and she humbled herself at His feet.

In Luke 10:39, we find her sitting at Jesus' feet, hearing His word. Her sister, Martha, was busy serving their physical needs, but Mary was more interested in hearing what Jesus had to say. She wanted to learn of Him, ask questions, find answers for her life. This takes time. It takes undivided attention. It's a real discipline to be able to give ourselves to listening to another person, when, often, we would rather be active physically. But, Mary, out of love for her Master, was willing to discipline herself to meditate upon His word as He spoke to her.

Perhaps because she had spent time listening to Jesus, Mary had come to know Him as her Lord. When Jesus came to Bethany after her brother Lazarus died, Mary ran out to meet Him, and fell at His feet in adoration. She was glad to see Him, and demonstrated her love and affection by humbling herself at His feet. She was not thanking Him for anything; indeed, she felt that He had come too late to help her brother. She was acknowledging Him for who He was, her Lord, Master and friend. What follows is one of the most poignant scenes in all Scripture. Mary began to cry and Jesus, deeply moved by her tears, wept with her. Even though he knew that He would raise her brother from the dead, He had compassion on Mary as she wept at His feet.

Mary anointed Jesus' feet with ointment, then wiped them with her hair. This is the third record we have of Mary at Jesus' feet. To honor Jesus for the return of Lazarus from the grave, a feast had been prepared for the rejoicing friends in the house of Simon, a leper who had been healed also by Jesus. Here, as on other occasions, Mary did not speak; her actions spoke for her. She got up from the table, took a precious box of spikenard, and anointed Jesus' feet in gratefulness for what He had done. She thought nothing of using this costly gift in this way, even though others in the room felt that she was very wasteful. Jesus appreciated the fragrance of this perfume, for it signified to Him the sweet aroma of Mary's worship. He appreciated her sacrifice, her love. He also knew that within a few days He would be dead. Though she did not know it, Mary was even now preparing His body for burial. This act of Mary's so moved Him that He said, "wheresoever this gospel shall be preached throughout the whole world, this also that she hath done shall be spoken of for a memorial of her" (Mark 14:9). She humbled herself and God exalted her in due time.

Do we humble ourselves before the feet of Jesus today? Do we, like Mary, take the time to sit at His feet and meditate on His word?

Do we prostrate ourselves before Him in adoration and worship? Can we, figuratively at least, fall before Him in times of grief and sorrow and let Him minister to us?

Do we anoint the feet of Jesus? Is giving a cup of cold water in His name, and caring for the least of those in need, a way of showing Him how much we love Him? Can we bless and adore Him with our tears of gratefulness for what He has done in our lives?

Someone has said that when Mary sat at Jesus' feet to listen to Him, she came to know Him as Prophet. When she fell at His feet in grief and humility, she knew Him as the sympathizing High Priest. When she anointed Him with the costly perfume in love and adoration, she recognized Him as King.

Can we today know Jesus as Prophet, as Priest, as King, by putting ourselves at the feet of Jesus?

Dear Jesus, I want to be like Mary and find meaning in my life at your feet. Help me to discipline myself to a time of listening to your word every day. Cause me to desire to praise you often, for you are worthy of all glory and honor and you have created me for your pleasure. I pray also that you show me how I can bless you, by ministering to others in your name. I want to humble myself before you and learn of you. Amen.

MARTHA

A WOMAN GIVEN TO HOSPITALITY
Luke 10:38-42; John 11:20-27; Rom. 12:10-13

> Let brotherly love continue. Be not forgetful to
> entertain strangers: for thereby some have enter-
> tained angels unawares.   Heb. 13:1, 2

Martha lived in Bethany with her brother Lazarus and her
sister Mary. It was a comfortable home, often full of
houseguests. Because Bethany was only a short distance
from Jerusalem, their home was an ideal base for Jesus when
He came into the area.

He often stayed in this home, particularly near the end of
His earthly ministry. It was a refuge for Him, where He
could receive comfort from those who loved Him as the
antagonism toward Him mounted. Here, He was safely
outside the city limits of Jerusalem, yet close enough to go
into the city for the work He had to do there. And, because
Bethany is located at the edge of the Mount of Olives, and
thus near the Garden of Gethsemane, He could retreat often
to be alone with God.

Martha was the perfect hostess. She not only cooked good
meals and kept the house spic and span, but she made her
guests feel at home. She was alert to their personal needs.
She, as well as her sister Mary, spent much time with Jesus,

meeting His earthly needs and benefiting from His ministry.

Martha made sure her guests felt welcome. We find an example of this at the time of her brother Lazarus' death. She took the initiative and got up and ran out to meet Jesus when she heard that He was approaching Bethany. Her sister and those who had come to mourn stayed in the house. She was the first to hear Jesus say that her brother would rise again. He, Jesus, was the resurrection and the life; whosoever believed on Him would never die.

It was in this home in Bethany that Jesus and His disciples met for dinner just before His triumphal entry into Jerusalem. Again, Martha served the meal, at which time Mary anointed His feet. It was a happy occasion, for Lazarus, who had been dead, sat at the table with them. Because of this, many people dropped by the house; they wanted to see not only Jesus, but Lazarus as well! (John 12:1-9). To a hostess, this meant offering them something to drink and a place to sit, at the very least. It meant cleaning up afterwards and putting things back in order.

It's interesting to observe that neither Martha nor Mary is mentioned as being at the crucifixion or resurrection, unless they were among the women who watched from afar off (Mark 15:40). More than likely, the women who had followed Jesus from Galilee (Luke 23:55), including His own mother, stayed at the house of Mary, Martha and Lazarus in Bethany during this crucial time. Martha probably spent much time at home preparing meals, doing laundry, and making the house a haven of rest. With the heart of a true servant, she probably ministered to the physical needs of many persons during these days of much anxiety. And she did it in her home.

What a ministry is involved in providing hospitality! As any woman knows, it takes time and preparation to entertain even the most casual guest. Someone has to shop, prepare the meals, make the beds, and see that the house is in order. It's a marvelous opportunity of service for women, as we entertain visiting speakers, friends, or even strangers in temporary need of a place to stay. It's a ministry often unnoticed, but an opportunity of real satisfaction for the one who provides, as well as the one who benefits.

Dear God, thank you for giving me, as a woman, that satisfaction of doing detailed, mundane duties that come with being a good hostess. I praise you for the beds I make, the meals I plan, the laundry I do to benefit my own family, as well as the guests you send my way. Help me to be a Martha, a willing servant, knowing that I may be entertaining angels unawares, or even you as that unseen guest. I am grateful to be your servant. Amen.

THE MOTHER OF
JAMES AND JOHN
A WOMAN WHO WAS
ASKED THE QUESTION EVERY
DISCIPLE MUST FACE
Matt. 20:20-28; John 15:18-20; 1 Pet. 4:13-19

> Yea, and all that will live godly in Christ Jesus
> shall suffer persecution.   2 Tim. 3:12

The mother of James and John was also the wife of
Zebedee (we are told in Matthew 4:21 that he was their
father). From this Scripture, it seems likely that Zebedee
raised his sons with a consciousness of the coming Messiah,
for when Jesus called James and John to follow Him, they
immediately left their father and their fishing nets. Not all
fathers would have let this happen so easily!

Some authorities believe that the wife of Zebedee was the
woman also referred to as Salome, one of the women who
followed Jesus to his death and then came to the tomb to
anoint His body. Whether or not she was this Salome, she,
too, must have joined her husband in allowing her sons to
follow Jesus.

It was not easy to let their sons go, especially to follow
someone whom they had only briefly seen and heard

themselves. As their relationship with the Master grew, James and John shared with their parents the things that happened in Jesus' ministry, as well as many of the teachings He was sharing with them.

When Jesus' popularity grew, this mother became ambitious for her sons. She knew that they were among His closest disciples and she felt sure that, when Jesus truly ruled in His kingdom, He would want her sons to have positions of honor. She did not understand the kingdom of which Jesus spoke, nor did she know what she would be asking for her sons.

However, one day, on the road to Jerusalem, after Jesus had told His disciples that He would be crucified and then resurrected, the mother of James and John decided that this was the time to make her request known.

She said to Jesus, "Grant that these my two sons may sit, the one on thy right hand, and the other on the left, in thy kingdom." Jesus responded with a question each of us must consider when we decide to follow Him and to be a part of His kingdom. He asked, "Are ye able to drink of the cup that I shall drink of, and to be baptized with the baptism that I am baptized with?" In other words, are we prepared to face the cup of suffering and the baptism of fire which will come into our lives?

There is much teaching on the inheritance we gain when we become children of the King. It is true that much has been accomplished for our benefit. We can claim salvation for our souls, healing for our bodies, and the fulfillment of every promise of God in His Word. He wants us to believe Him, and He will supply our every need through Christ Jesus. We become seated with Him in heavenly places; we will reign with Him eternally.

There is another aspect to following Jesus that we do not like to face. We will have suffering and persecution. Jesus did. Though He was the Son of God, He had to suffer. He was persecuted; He was misunderstood. Just before the mother of James and John asked her question, He had told His followers that He would be tried, mocked, betrayed and put to death. He was made perfect through this suffering (Heb. 2:10).

The Bible tells us to expect persecution, the cup of suffering, and the baptism of fire. Timothy reminds us that all who live godly in Christ Jesus shall suffer persecution (2 Tim. 3:12). John the Baptist said that Jesus will baptize us with the Holy Ghost and with fire, by which God will purge us (Matt. 3:11-12). Paul tells us that all the hay, wood, and stubble in our lives will be burned; our works will be revealed by fire (1 Cor. 3:12-13). 1 Peter says not to be surprised when fiery trials come upon us (1 Pet. 4:12). We, like Jesus, need suffering to perfect us.

How do we respond to trials and tribulation? Jesus gives us specific instructions in the Sermon on the Mount (Matt. 5:44). "Love your enemies, bless them that curse you, do good to them that hate you, and pray for them which despitefully use you."

Our natural tendency is to either retaliate in like manner or ignore the whole situation. But Jesus gives us positive commands, things to do in the midst of suffering and fire. In doing these things, we become more like Him.

The mother of James and John wanted a shortcut to honor and position for her sons. But Jesus knew what lay ahead for them, as leaders in the early Church. He knew that to whom much was given, much would be required.

Just like this mother, we all want shortcuts—instant healing, easy money, and positions of honor without cost. We want to avoid the pain, the frustration, the work involved. Jesus didn't have these shortcuts and neither will His followers.

In fact, Paul came to the place where he could say, "I take pleasure in infirmities, in reproaches, in necessities, in persecutions, in distresses for Christ's sake: for when I am weak, then am I strong" (2 Cor. 12:10). He learned how to respond positively to suffering, to let God form in Him the nature of Jesus through it.

As we seek our place in His Kingdom today, what is our response to Jesus' question: "Are ye able to drink of the cup that I shall drink of, and be baptized with the baptism that I am baptized with?"

Dear Lord, help me to glory in tribulations also, knowing that tribulation works patience; and patience, experience; and experience, hope. Help me to bless, to love, to pray when I am hurt—to become more like you, through suffering. Amen.

THE WIDOW WITH TWO MITES

A WOMAN WHO GAVE
HER ALL TO THE LORD

Mark 12:41-44; Matt. 6:19-21; 2 Cor. 8:1-5

> One thing thou lackest: go thy way, sell
> whatsoever thou hast, and give to the poor, and
> thou shalt have treasure in heaven: and come,
> take up the cross, and follow me.   Mark 10:21

Jesus sat down on the stone bench, weary. He wanted a few minutes alone. As people came in and out of the temple, He rested as He thought about the morning and how exhausting it had been. In fact, it was only one day of a very busy week, and He still had much to do.

Only two days before, He had come into Jerusalem on a colt, with people laying palm branches before Him, and acclaiming Him as the King who had come in the name of the Lord. It had been a happy occasion, though a sad one, too. It was happy because it was a taste of things to come; it was sad because He knew what would happen by the end of the week.

Today He had spent most of His time in the temple. He wanted to be with as many people as He could; He had so much to say and so little time left. First, His authority had been questioned by the chief priests. After He answered them, He shared a parable that exposed their attitude. This made them so angry that they would have seized Him then, had they not feared the people.

Next, the Pharisees tried to catch Him by questioning Him about submission to government. Then the Sadducees, as usual, asked Him contrived questions about resurrection. As the scribes joined the discussion, He told the crowd to beware of them and their hypocrisy. Everything He said seemed to offend someone. Many people had heard Him *speak,* and He wondered how many actually heard what He *said.*

As Jesus reflected on the events of the day, He watched the men and women file by the offering box. It was Paschal Week and people from everywhere poured into the court of the temple with their offerings. Receptacles for these gifts lined the walls. The bench on which Jesus was sitting happened to be across from one of these receptacles. Many wealthy men came by and made no pretense of concealing the amount of their offerings.

Jesus noticed a little old lady hobbling up to the offering box. She walked slowly and seemed to be mumbling to herself. He couldn't hear her voice, but from the way she lifted her eyes toward heaven, He knew she was praying as she prepared to drop in her gift. Though no one else paid attention to her, Jesus saw her drop two mites into the box. He breathed a blessing upon her, realizing she had just given all that she had. Her two coins were more than what was given by anyone else that day, for she had given her all—one hundred percent. His eyes followed her, as she made her way out through the courtyard and disappeared down the street. The little widow woman had just contributed the largest gift of the day—in His eyes.

Jesus remembered how, earlier in His ministry, a rich young ruler had come to Him, wanting to know how he could obtain eternal life. He was a devout young man, having obeyed all the commandments from his youth. Jesus recalled how, when He told the ruler that he needed to sell all that he had, take up his cross and follow Him, the young man had gone away sorrowfully. He couldn't do it; he wasn't ready to give up everything to follow Jesus.

Today Jesus had seen one person who had come to that place of commitment. He had seen a woman who had very little, yet was willing to give even that. Somebody had heard His message; He was grateful to know that His teaching had not fallen on deaf ears.

Jesus spent a few moments thinking. Why were people reluctant to give up earthly possessions and worldly involvement to follow Him, when they actually had so much more to gain? Were they afraid to trust God to supply every need? Jesus grieved as He realized how blind people still were after all He had taught them.

His eyes scanned the crowd for the disciples. Sure enough, He saw some of them standing over in a corner, talking among themselves. His strength returned; He had a job to complete! He called out, "Peter, John, Thomas—gather the rest of the disciples and come here! I have a very important message that I need to share with you!"

While He waited for them to come, Jesus thought again of the little old woman, and prayed that God would truly bless her life this day.

Dear God, thank you for showing me that I have not yet come to the place of wanting to sell all that I have, give to the poor, take up my cross, and follow you. Help me, O Lord, to become willing to do what you ask, to trust you completely that you may truly become my Lord and Master. Amen.

PILATE'S WIFE

A WOMAN WHO WAS GIVEN
A MESSAGE IN A DREAM

Matt. 27:11-24; Job 33:14-17

And it shall come to pass in the last days, saith
God, I will pour out of my Spirit upon all flesh:
and your sons and your daughters shall prophesy,
and your young men shall see visions, and your old
men shall dream dreams.   Acts 2:17

From Genesis to Revelation, God used dreams and
visions as a means of communicating with man. Only once
was a dream given to a woman; all that we know about this
dream is contained in one verse (Matt. 27:19). Here we see
that Pilate's wife tried to warn her husband concerning
Jesus, because of a dream she had.

Pilate was the procurator of Judea and, as was the custom
of governors, probably resided in Caesarea but went to
Jerusalem to keep order at the time of the national feasts.
Pilate's wife accompanied him to Jerusalem at the time of
the Passover, which coincided with Jesus' arrest and trial.

Here, Jesus was brought before Pilate, who asked Him if
He was, indeed, the King of the Jews. Pilate was surprised
when Jesus did not respond as he expected. In order to

205

appease the crowd, he decided to give them a choice between releasing Jesus or a notable prisoner, Barabbas.

It was at this point, as he sat down upon the judgment seat, that Pilate's wife sent him a message. She warned him not to have anything to do with Jesus, because of a dream she had had about Him.

We have no way of knowing what was in this dream, though it may have been like a nightmare; she said that she had suffered much through it. Had she seen Jesus beaten, humiliated and crucified? Had she heard Jesus himself speak to her from the cross, pronouncing judgment on Pilate for letting Him, an innocent man, die? Perhaps God revealed to her, through a glimpse of the resurrection, that Jesus truly was the Son of God. Whatever happened in her dream, it troubled her enough to send a message to Pilate, warning him to have nothing to do with Jesus.

Why was this dream not given to Pilate himself? After all, he was the one who could have done something about it! We are not sure that he would have listened to God speak through a dream, because Pilate feared the people more than he feared God. He let circumstances rule the situation by default; he did not take the responsibility that was his, and washed his hands of the whole affair.

We are told that, in the last days, dreams and visions will occur as God pours out His Spirit upon all flesh. He can often give specific guidance and insights in this way when our minds are not in control. When we are awake, we usually think so logically that we can't hear what God might be saying, unless we, by His Spirit, have learned to listen to His still, small voice.

We must realize, however, that not all dreams contain messages from God. Physical stimuli cause some dreams. They can be triggered by an incident that happened to us during the day, or even by the food we ate for a bedtime snack!

The devil can also influence our dreams. This is especially obvious when the dream produces real fear, for Timothy tells us that "God hath not given us the spirit of fear; but of power, and of love, and of a sound mind" (2 Tim. 1:7). Pilate's wife had a dream that troubled her, but it gave her a fear of the Lord, which is different than the panicky fear provoked by Satan.

How do we know when our dreams are from God? As with any message from the Lord (such as prophecy), it should be tested. God always agrees with himself. He does not give one message and then completely contradict himself in another message. Paul says, "In the mouth of two or three witnesses shall every word be established" (2 Cor. 13:1). Does the dream agree with God's Word? How do other believers witness to it? We can also ask for the gifts of discernment, wisdom and knowledge.

We can also recall what God has been saying to us through other means; God rarely gives specific instructions without preparing the hearer previously in some way. We have peace when God speaks.

Finally, we do not need to make a dream come to pass. If it is of God, He will do it. We won't need to try to make it happen.

As Christians, we should be open to God's direction through dreams, but these dreams should never be our only source of guidance.

If, like Pilate's wife, we feel that we have heard from God through a dream, and it has passed all of the tests of a true message, we can pass it on to those concerned. If they do not heed the message, that is their problem, not ours. God warned Pilate through a dream that He gave to his wife, and the course of history was set because Pilate chose not to listen to what had been revealed to her.

Thank you, Lord, for the means of communication you have with us. Thank you, too, for your living Word which cannot be broken. I especially appreciate living in these days when your gifts to the Body are being poured out by your Holy Spirit. Help me to learn to know your voice in whatever way you choose to speak to me. Amen.

SAPPHIRA

A WOMAN WHO REAPED
THE CONSEQUENCES OF SIN

Acts 4:32-5:11; Rev. 20:11-15

Let no man say when he is tempted, I am tempted of
God: for God cannot be tempted with evil, neither
tempteth he any man: But every man is tempted,
when he is drawn away of his own lust, and enticed.
Then, when lust hath conceived, it bringeth forth
sin: and sin, when it is finished, bringeth forth
death.   James 1:13-15

Sapphira, the wife of Ananias, was one of the Christians
of the early church. After the Holy Spirit had been poured
out upon the one hundred and twenty in the upper room, the
Lord moved mightily through miracles, signs and wonders.
Over three thousand came to the Lord in just one day after
hearing Peter preach under the power and anointing of the
Holy Spirit. Perhaps Sapphira was one of these.

The first converts were so totally committed to God that
they sold their possessions and held all things in common.
They brought all their own material resources and laid them
at the apostles' feet, so that those who lacked would be
provided for. Luke notes that these early Christians were of

one heart and of one soul; they had complete agreement in this arrangement of sharing with each other. This oneness of heart and soul had to have come from the Lord, for only He could bring about such a unity!

Sapphira and her husband also sold a possession, but they schemed to hold back some of their profit. They did not tell anyone, thinking that it was a secret between themselves. They were agreed with each other, but not with God. He wanted them to be one in Him (John 17:11), one in His Spirit (Gal. 5:16), and to have the mind of Christ (Phil. 2:5). They were one with each other, but not one in the Spirit of the Lord!

Some justify Sapphira's actions, saying that she simply submitted to her husband, but the Word doesn't tell us that she felt differently than he did. She didn't submit to her husband; she just "went along with the game." In true submission, the wife has the responsibility of bringing before her husband what she feels is right and what the Lord would have her do, especially if it is contrary to what the husband is asking of her. Her conscience is then clear, whatever her husband decides, even though she may need to submit to his will after all. Submission is active, not passive.

Sapphira did not search her own heart. If she had, she would have found lust, deceit, or some other sin that she was trying to cover up. Maybe she didn't see sin for what it really is. Perhaps she just said to herself: "God is love; He'll forgive me anyway. He knows that we've given most of our profit to the group. A little bit for ourselves isn't going to harm anybody. What they don't know won't hurt them!" Though she was a believer, she did not see the necessity of daily repentance and cleansing of all unrighteousness by the blood of Jesus.

Significantly, Sapphira and her husband, Ananias, faced their judgment separately. Though in their sin they had been in complete agreement, each had to face Peter and the other apostles alone, and give account individually. Each died without knowing what happened to the other.

Likewise, each one of us will stand before God alone. It will be a sad Judgment Day for us if we think that we can deceive God. Like Sapphira, we, too, will have no one to blame; we must answer for ourselves!

Dear God, I thank you for saving me, for revealing to me my need of a Savior. Help me to hate sin and be willing to repent of the wrong attitudes and motives that I recognize within myself. Teach me true submission as you also teach me to fear you, to know that you are a just God as well as a loving Father. Amen.

DORCAS

A WOMAN WHO
DID MANY GOOD WORKS

Acts 9:36-42; James 2:14-18

> Pure religion and undefiled before God and the
> Father is this, To visit the fatherless and widows
> in their affliction, and to keep himself unspotted
> from the world.   James 1:27

Dorcas (or Tabitha, as she was also called) was a disciple
in the early church. She lived in Joppa, a town on the
Mediterranean seacoast, where there was a large group of
believers.

One day Dorcas became ill and died. The women who had
been attending her wrapped her body and laid it upon a bed;
then they sent for Peter, who was in nearby Lydda.

When Peter arrived, he found these women, mostly
widows, standing around Dorcas' body, weeping. They had
lost not only a good friend, but a fellow worker as well. They
showed him all the garments that Dorcas had made for
people, and also recounted the many good works she had
done. Peter finally had to send the whole group from the
room in order to be alone with God. He knelt down and
prayed, then turned to her body and said, "Tabitha, arise."

With these words, Dorcas opened her eyes, looked at Peter, and sat up!

The rejoicing was great when Peter presented Dorcas to the mourners. The news spread throughout Joppa, and many believed in the Lord because of this miracle.

Dorcas was a very practical person. When people needed clothes, she made them. Perhaps the widows gathered about her during her last illness were part of a sewing circle she had formed to make clothes for orphans and poor people! She was not in business to make a profit, but to serve her Lord. By raising her to life again, God extended her ministry of good works.

The Body today needs people like Dorcas, who are willing to use their creative talents for God. The poor still need the clothing we can make and share. Hospitals can use volunteers of all kinds. What nursing home wouldn't be thrilled to have someone offer to read to the residents, to write letters for them, or help with a simple crafts program? Senior citizens' groups always are on the lookout for drivers to take the elderly to the doctor or the grocery store. Juvenile homes often need women to help teach girls homemaking skills, such as cooking and sewing. Church youth groups continually need adults to help in their programs in some way. How about taking the children of working or single parents on an outing or caring for a new baby, so that the homebound mother can have a few hours to herself.

We are tempted in our Christian walk to think of ourselves, of how we are getting fed, of what ways God is providing and blessing our own lives. We forget that He said that pure religion and undefiled before him is to visit the fatherless and widows in their afflictions. We have a practical responsibility to others, especially to those who are less fortunate.

God needed Dorcas in her day so much that He extended her life. God still needs our good works; He needs people like Dorcas today.

Dear Lord, thank you for giving me talents that I can use in service to you. Help me not to seek glory for myself, but rather lose myself that others may benefit. I am grateful that you are a creative God, that you made no two of us alike, and that you have a unique place for me in your Body. I love you and appreciate what you have done for me. I want to share your love with others in a very practical way. Show me how, I pray. Amen.

RHODA

A YOUNG WOMAN WHO HAD GOOD NEWS THAT WAS NOT RECEIVED

Acts 12:1-17; Luke 24:1-11

And some believed the things which were
spoken, and some believed not.   Acts 28:24

Have you ever tried to share a supernatural work of God
with someone who would not believe you? Have you
wondered how to convince them that you were telling the
truth? If so, you can identify with Rhoda. This is her story.

Persecution had hit the early church. Herod himself
attacked the leadership by killing James, John's brother.
When he saw it pleased the Jews, he put Peter into prison,
intending to kill him also.

Believers gathered to pray at the home of John Mark's
mother, Mary. In fact, we are told that prayer was made
without ceasing by the church on behalf of Peter (Acts 12:5).
God moved by sending an angel to miraculously free Peter
from prison. Immediately, he went to Mary's house where he
knocked at the outer entrance, eager to show his friends
what the Lord had done. Rhoda, the servant girl, ran to open
the door. When she recognized Peter's voice, she was so
overjoyed that she neglected to open the door before running

217

back to the group to share the good news with them! And what was the response of those who had been fervently praying for the release of their leader? They accused Rhoda of being mad! Rhoda's good news was not received and Peter was left standing outside the house!

Several years earlier, it had been Peter, along with the other disciples, who had not believed a report of good news. Some women who had gone to the tomb of Jesus to anoint His body following the crucifixion had found, instead, two angels who told them that Jesus had risen from the dead. They, in their excitement, had run to tell the disciples what had happened, but they did not believe them either! "And their words seemed to them as idle tales, and they believed them not" (Luke 24:11).

There may be times when we, too, will and should question reports of supernatural events, but, for now, let us just consider what our attitude should be toward those who do not accept a testimony that we might have. These may include husbands who do not share our walk with the Lord, children who are turned off by "religion," fellow employees who avoid us, or neighbors who are very much in the world. Or, as Rhoda found, they may be Christians who do not respond with belief to answered prayer.

One of the things that we may need to do is fight a spiritual battle, binding the work of Satan in people's minds so that they may be open to the truth. We know from Scripture that Satan as "the god of this world hath blinded the minds of them which believe not, lest the light of the glorious gospel of Christ, who is the image of God, should shine unto them" (2 Cor. 4:4).

Also, our lives need to be consistent with the Word of God. For instance, we are given a word to wives in 1 Peter 3:1 which says they will win their husbands not by their words, but by their behavior. And, in the Sermon on the Mount,

Jesus tells us to love our enemies, to bless them that curse us, to do good to them that hate us, to pray for them which despitefully use us and persecute us (Matt. 5:44).

Our natural inclination, on the other hand, is to try to make ourselves heard. But we cannot open ears; only God can do that. Long ago, the Lord told Moses: ". . . I will make them (the people) hear my words, that they may learn to fear me all the days that they shall live upon the earth, and that they may teach their children" (Deut. 4:10).

Rhoda could not make the others believe what she knew to be true, but Acts 12:15 says that "she constantly affirmed that it was even so." She continued to testify in spite of ridicule. And Peter continued to knock on the door until it was opened, proving what Rhoda had said was true.

When we witness of something we know to be of God, we do not have to defend it or be intimidated by those who refuse to believe it. Rather, our job is to use the weapons of spiritual warfare, to love, bless, pray, and do good. Then God, in His own time and His own way, will reveal himself and perform His Word.

Dear God, I realize that I am so impatient with those who will not hear me, especially when I share the wonderful things you do in my life. Please help me to love them with your love. I will allow you to open their hearts and ears. By your grace and mercy, keep me in your truth. Amen.

LYDIA

A WOMAN WHO WAS BOTH A SUCCESSFUL BUSINESSWOMAN AND A MISSIONARY

Acts 16:9-15, 40; Phil. 1:1-5, 15

Be kindly affectioned one to another with brotherly love; in honour preferring one another; Not slothful in business; fervent in spirit; serving the Lord.   Rom. 12:10, 11

God works in mysterious ways to accomplish His will. When we are led by His Spirit, we will often find ourselves in places and situations which surprise us, for our ways and thoughts are not His ways and thoughts.

The apostle Paul had such an experience. He wanted to revisit some of the places in Asia Minor where he had preached; but God had other plans. He wanted Paul to start a work in Europe, and gave Paul a night vision while he was in the city of Troas. In this vision, a man appeared and asked them to come over to Macedonia (Greece). The next day, under the direction of the Holy Spirit, Paul and his companions, sailed for Philippi, the most important city of Macedonia.

Now, when Paul arrived there, he didn't have a ready-made congregation to work with; instead, he went down by the nearby river where the Jews met to pray. When talking with some of the women who had come to the riverside to worship, he met Lydia.

Lydia was not a Greek, but had come from a Greek colony in Asia Minor. Her home was in Thyatira, a city well known for its dyes. Her work had led her to Philippi, where she had a thriving business as a seller of purple. This meant that she sold garments of silk to the nobility.

Purple is used several times in Scripture as a sign of royalty. Luke describes a rich man who was clothed in purple and fine linen (Luke 16:19). When the mock trial of Jesus was held, the soldiers clothed Him with purple, put a crown of thorns upon His head, and saluted Him as "King of the Jews" (Mark 15:17).

Lydia was not only a good businesswoman, but she was a proselyte, "one who worshipped God." When Paul began to explain to her how the Messiah had already come, she wanted to know more. It wasn't long before she and her whole household claimed Jesus as their own Lord and Savior and were baptized.

Lydia had a large house and she invited Paul and his team to stay with her. Most Bible scholars agree that the church of Philippi began in her home.

This church in Philippi is known for its missionary spirit. When he was imprisoned in Rome, Paul wrote to this church and thanked them for their generous support when all other churches had forsaken him (Phil. 4:15, 16).

Lydia may have been the very one who most exemplified this missionary spirit in this church of Philippi. As mentioned before, she was from Thyatira, one of the seven churches for whom John was given a message (Rev. 2:18-29). Yet we don't know if Paul visited here on any of his missionary journeys. Could it be that Lydia, burdened with love for her friends and family back home, became a missionary to them? Perhaps through business contacts, she witnessed for the Lord, telling how the Messiah came, was crucified, buried, and then rose again to save them.

She could have easily been the very person Paul had in mind when he later encouraged the Romans to be "not slothful in business; fervent in spirit; serving the Lord" (Rom. 12:11). Lydia was a good businesswoman, yet she also served the Lord with a fervent missionary spirit.

Thank you, Lord, for the talents you've given me. Help me to use them not only to benefit others or myself, but you as well. Give me a burden for souls, that I may share the good news with those you put me in contact with—whether at home, at my job, in my family, or among my friends. Amen.

PRISCILLA

A WOMAN WHO LABORED
TO BUILD UP OTHERS

Acts 18:1-3, 18-26; Rom. 16:3, 4; 1 Cor. 16:19; 2 Tim. 4:19

> I have planted, Apollos watered; but God gave
> the increase . . . . For we are laborers together
> with God.   1 Cor. 3:6, 9a

Priscilla and Aquila, Aquila and Priscilla—even Paul
thought of them together so much that he interchanged their
names when speaking of them. What a team this husband
and wife must have made! They were always recognized as a
couple in what they did—whether it was entertaining in their
home, making tents, or ministering to people!

Priscilla and Aquila were Jews who had been deported
from Rome, where they were tentmakers. They settled in
Cornith, where they made a new life for themselves by
re-establishing their business. Here they met Paul, who often
stayed in their home whenever he returned to this city. They
had a mutual occupation, tentmaking, but they were also
fellow believers and traveled with Paul as he ministered in
various other cities.

On one of their journeys, Paul left Priscilla and Aquila in
Ephesus while he went on to Antioch and Jerusalem. While

here, they listened to the eloquent Apollos teach, and realized he was not aware of the full gospel of Jesus, since he was teaching only the baptism of John. They took him aside and shared with him the baptism in the name of the Lord Jesus, and the baptism in the Holy Spirit. (Acts 19:1-6 illustrates that these doctrines had not been a part of Apollos' teaching in Ephesus.)

God used both Aquila and Priscilla to minister His Word. The beautiful thing is there there appeared to be no competition between them, nor were they jealous of Apollos. They encouraged him instead of tearing him down. They realized that each one has a contribution to make, and that God needs each part of the Body for a particular function. Priscilla and Aquila were also mutually dependent upon each other, and their ministry really flowed as they acted together. They made an ideal team.

Priscilla was a true helper in other areas of her life as well. She was a co-worker with her husband in every way. She willingly helped earn their living, making tents. She traveled with Aquila, ministering where she could, though this meant living in all kinds of accommodations; yet wherever they were, their home was open to fellow believers for worship and ministry, as well as to Paul, who was a frequent house guest.

Priscilla was flexible, and she desired to follow the Lord's leading, wherever it took her. She was willing to give up her own rights and separate identity to be with her husband, and to go where the Lord called him.

Priscilla was that rare individual who sought ways to encourage others and help them in their work, rather than build herself up at others' expense, or forsake responsibility altogether. She helped her husband, both in business and at home. She helped Paul and other teachers of the gospel. We have no idea how many others she helped in the process when as she opened her home as a meeting place for the church.

Paul admonishes us, as Christians and children of the light, to comfort ourselves together and to edify (or build up) one another (1 Thess. 5:11). This was Priscilla's ministry as a helper, and she did it well.

Dear God, help me to accept the place in which you have put me. Even though you sometimes put me in strange places away from family and friends, I know that you have a plan for my life and will give me new relationships and new paths to follow. Help me to be willing to do what you ask in my job, in my relationship with my husband, in my home, and in whatever tasks you have for me. Let me be an encouragement to others. Amen.

PHEBE
A WOMAN WHO SERVED OTHERS
Rom. 16:1, 2; John 12:26; Isa. 52:13

> For, brethren, ye have been called unto liberty;
> only use not liberty for an occasion to the flesh,
> but by love serve one another.   Gal. 5:13

Phebe is mentioned in only two sentences in the Bible, yet what a tribute they contain! Paul calls Phebe "our sister" and "a servant of the church." She had helped many, including him.

Phebe lived in the city of Cenchrea, a busy seaport nine miles east of Corinth. She served as courier of the letter Paul sent to the church at Rome. At the close of this letter, he reminded the believers in Rome that she was a fellow sister in the Lord, and he commended her to them and asked that they help her in any way that was necessary.

Phebe was a servant in the church of Cenchrea. (We would probably call her a deaconess in some of our churches.) She probably watched over women converts, and saw that they were properly disciplined. She cared for the sick, doing those little things that mean so much to one who is ill—providing meals, running errands, seeing that the children were cared for. She likely visited those who were suffering in prison, bringing them food as well as news that would comfort and encourage them. Then, there were functional duties to perform in preparation for worship, such as seeing that the bread was baked and the wine made available for the group to celebrate the Lord's Supper.

It's interesting to note that the word used here for "servant" is, in Greek, *diakonos,* one who runs errands or is an attendant, such as a waiter at a meal.

Those of us who have eaten at restaurants are aware of when we have good waiters and when we don't. The waiter's attitude often makes the difference in the kind of service we receive. If the waiter has the heart of a servant, we enjoy our meal and feel truly waited upon. On the other hand, if he does his job out of a mere sense of duty, we feel cheated and do not experience good service.

As servants of the church, we too have a choice. Will we serve out of love or because of duty? Phebe must have had a servant's heart; she went beyond the call of duty. It may have been out of her way to go to Rome and look up certain people there. Perhaps she had to take extra time away from her home to deliver this letter for Paul.

As mothers, we face a choice every day. Will we cook the meals, make the beds and do the laundry because our job demands it? If we do, then we really aren't serving anyone (except perhaps ourselves, so we won't feel guilty). If, however, our attitude is one of love, meekness, and patience, our family will be served by having their needs met, and they will see Jesus in us as well.

In Isaiah we have a description of the true servant that God would send to His people (Isa. 50-53). We all recognize Jesus, the servant who gave His own life out of love for us (chapter 53). He not only served man during His earthly life, but He served us in death that we might have eternal life.

Soon after His triumphal entry into Jerusalem, certain Greeks came to Philip and Andrew, desiring to see Jesus.

It was to them that Jesus not only gave a hint of His approaching death, but also described the reward of those who would be His servants, when He said, "If any man serve me, let him follow me; and where I am, there shall also my servant be: if any man serve me, him will my Father honour" (John 12:26).

Serving the Lord is commitment to doing His will as we follow Him. What should be our attitude when we serve? Paul tells us that "the servant of the Lord must not strive; but be gentle unto all men, apt to teach, patient; In meekness instructing those that oppose themselves" (2 Tim. 2:24, 25). God wants us to be servants, but more than this, to have the *hearts* of servants, to be gentle, patient, and meek. To do this, we allow the Servant Jesus to fill our hearts with His love, so that He can serve through us.

Dear Heavenly Father, as you loved me so much to send your Son to die for me, help me to die to my own self in love for you. Teach me to express this love by serving those around me, particularly those in my family and in your family, the Church. Give me a right attitude in serving that you may be seen in me. Thank you, Lord Jesus, my Master. Amen.

EUODIAS AND SYNTYCHE

TWO WOMEN WHO
WERE NOT OF THE SAME MIND

Phil. 4:2; 1 Cor. 3:1-9, 22

> Finally, be ye all of one mind, having compassion
> one of another, love as brethren, be pitiful, be
> courteous: Not rendering evil for evil, or railing
> for railing: but contrariwise blessing; knowing
> that ye are thereunto called, that ye should
> inherit a blessing.   1 Pet. 3:8, 9

If Paul were alive today, he could probably write to
each Christian fellowship and say: "Ruth and Maxine,
you are hurting the whole Body of Christ by the division
you are creating among its members." Or, "Mary and
Norma, please learn to work with your leaders as well as with
each other." Or, "Connie and Debbie, do stop the bickering
and blaming one another that I hear is going on in your
group." Or, as he did long ago, "I beseech Euodias, and
beseech Syntyche, that they be of the same mind in the
Lord."

Paul had problems with quarrelsome women in his day;
the Body today suffers from the same thing. We still need
to heed the warning given two thousand years ago. We still

need to learn to love one another, and relate to each other as part of the same Body.

We have Scriptures which tell us to be of one mind (1 Pet. 3:8, 9), to dwell together in unity (Ps. 133:1), and to be one in the Spirit, as we have one Lord, one faith, one baptism (Eph. 4:4, 5). We know that in the early church that there were times when the believers were of one accord (Acts 2:46) and many people came to the Lord as a result. We also know that one of the seven abominations to the Lord is "he that soweth discord among the brethren" (Prov. 6:16-19).

The Bible doesn't tell us if Euodias and Syntyche ever reconciled, or how much their disagreement affected the rest of the Body. Paul felt that it was hindering the Lord's work enough to admonish them in his letter to their church.

Today, we need to hear Paul's challenge to them: how *does* one come into the same mind in the Lord with another person?

Let us take the problems of each of these pairs of modern women given at the beginning of this chapter and see if we can find an answer in the Word of God.

Ruth and Maxine caused division in the Body. This happened because each thought that her way was the right way. They forgot that the Body is one, that we are all members in it, though we each have different functions. The Corinthian church had begun to have this problem, too, when they began to follow men instead of Jesus. Various teachers had visited Corinth, preaching and baptizing. These converts then began to identify with the ones who had taught and baptized them; thus, some were of Cephas (Peter), some of Apollos, some of Paul—all were good men. They forgot the true Head of the Body, Jesus. So, Paul wrote to the Ruths and Maxines (as well as to the Toms and Bobs!) in Corinth: "Now I beseech you, brethren, by the name of the Lord Jesus Christ, that ye all speak the same thing, and that there be no divisions among you; but that ye be perfectly joined together in the same mind and in the same judgment" (1 Cor. 1:10). He continued that they were to be joined perfectly together in the same mind by looking to Jesus, not to the various men God had used to bring the gospel to them. Men were only God's messengers.

Mary and Norma's situation seems paradoxical. "Now learn about authority and submit to one another!" Paul might have said to them. Jesus is the Head of the Church, but God has also established a divine order in His Body, and we must learn to submit to one another, as well as to Him. The writer of Hebrews tells us to "remember them which have the rule over you, who have spoken unto you the word of God: whose faith follow, considering the end of their conversation" (Heb. 13:7). God has given authority to pastors, elders and husbands; and we, as women, need to learn to submit to them. Whenever differences of opinion rise among us, perhaps we, like Mary and Norma, need to ask ourselves the question: "Am I assuming authority that is really not mine?"

Perhaps the most common problem among women is illustrated by Connie and Debbie. There is probably no group of women immune from bickering, criticizing, or finding fault with one another. It's a part of our old nature that has not been dealt with. We have not learned to lay down our own rights, to esteem others better than ourselves. We have not learned to be servants and follow the pattern of Jesus, so that we can be of one spirit (Phil. 2:1-7). If we bicker, quarrel, argue, or speak evil, then we really are not fulfilling our calling as followers of Jesus Christ. Peter says that as part of our calling we must bless one another (1 Pet. 3:9); we must find ways to help others know the blessing of God in their lives. As Paul says, "There should be no schism in the body; but that the members should have the same care for one another" (1 Cor. 12:25)

Like Euodias and Syntyche, we are all laborers together with God. Each person has a function in this Body. We need to know our place in it and be in submission to authority. At the same time, as we allow Jesus to manifest himself through us, we can be that blessing to others that God has called us to be. Only then can we come into the same mind, for then we will have the mind of Jesus Christ.

Dear God, let the beauty of Jesus be seen in me today. Let me be willing to die to myself that you might shine through me. Lord, help me to know my place in your Body and to recognize the function others have in it as well. Give me a submissive spirit that I might learn to be of the same mind in you and with other believers. I thank you for calling me to bless others. Help me to share your blessing with at least one person today. Amen.

LOIS AND EUNICE

TWO WOMEN WHO WERE ABLE TO PASS THEIR FAITH ON TO THEIR CHILDREN

2 Tim. 1:1-8; Acts 16:1-3; 1 Cor. 7:14 (Amplified)

> Train up a child in the way he should go: and when he is old, he will not depart from it.   Prov. 22:6

Paul often called Timothy his "dearly beloved son." Though they were not blood relatives, there was a special bond between these two men; Paul took Timothy under his wing and discipled him in the way of the Lord.

Paul wasn't the first person to care for Timothy's spiritual welfare. The seed for the gift of God within him was planted early in his childhood by his grandmother Lois and his mother Eunice. Paul mentioned their "unfeigned faith" in the first epistle to Timothy. They were believers with whom Paul was acquainted; their strong faith had passed from mother to daughter to son.

Scripture doesn't tell us the name of Timothy's father. Luke does say that his father was a Greek, and evidently not a believer himself, though his wife, a Jewess, was (Acts 16:1).

In our day of broken and divided families, we sometimes despair, wondering how children can be given proper spiritual instruction without that divine order that is part of God's plan for families. God does want the father to be the priest of the household and instruct the children in the way of the Lord; the family functions best in this setting. But some households have just one parent who tries to raise children alone. God promises to be a father to the fatherless (Ps. 68:5). He will cover these children, if the single parents looks to Him for this protection. Single parents can see that their children receive instruction in the Word by being a part of a fellowship where the Scriptures are taught and by reading the Bible together at home. Much of what a child learns is by example. If he sees even one parent praying or trusting God to supply his needs, or sharing the work of the Lord in his own life, the child will be encouraged in his own faith in God.

But what about a home where one parent is a believer and the other isn't? In the case of Timothy's parents, Eunice still could have submitted to her husband. She still prayed and studied God's Word. By example, she taught much to Timothy. When even one member of a family trusts God, the rest of the family has God's attention.

The Bible gives several examples of this. Rahab's whole family was saved through her belief (Josh. 6:25). Lydia's whole household was saved through her faith and testimony (Acts 16:15). The Philippian jailer's whole household came to the Lord when he did (Acts 16:32-34). The family is God's workshop here on earth, where we receive training enabling us to establish the proper relationships in His family. We are children learning to obey our Father. We are the Bride learning to submit to the Bridegroom. God wants whole families in His family.

Both Lois and Eunice realized that raising a child in a Christian atmosphere does not automatically make that one a child of God. They taught Timothy to be a good, moral person, but, until he had accepted Jesus as his own personal Savior, he was not born into the family of God. At some point in his life, they had guided him to such a decision.

Lois and Eunice did not know how God would use Timothy and they probably had occasion to wonder if all they had taught him would be lost through pressures of the world. They had to believe that God would keep His hand upon Timothy, and rest in the knowledge that they had given him the best training they could.

What a blessing it is when families share in the faith, when one generation shares with another generation the Word of the Lord. It binds a family together and also strengthens each individual member.

Lois and Eunice must have known great satisfaction as they saw Timothy embrace their faith and watched as he, in turn, shared his faith with others.

Dear Heavenly Father, thank you for those godly people in my own family who influenced my life by their prayers, their examples, and the sharing of the faith. I do appreciate this heritage of mine. Help me to pass on my faith in you to my own children or children in my larger family my faith in you. Thank you, Father, for showing me how. Amen.

THE ELECT LADY

A WOMAN WHO RECEIVED
A LETTER FROM A FRIEND

2 John 1-13; 2 Tim. 3:1-7

> These things have I written unto you that believe
> on the name of the Son of God; that ye may know
> that ye have eternal life, and that ye may believe
> on the name of the Son of God.   1 John 5:13

Dear Elect Lady,

Over nineteen hundred years ago, I wrote a letter to a friend of mine, a woman who lived near Ephesus. She and her sister, as well as their children, were of great help to me. I especially appreciated her dedication to the Lord, and her kind hospitality to me. I called this friend of mine the Elect Lady, not only because she was one of God's elect people, but also because she was, in every respect, a real lady, in my opinion, and the ideal Christian woman. As her elder in the Lord, I desired to see her continue in the Way, so I wrote her a special letter giving a special warning.

This letter was later put into the canonized Scripture for all people to read. Actually, though some of the books of the Bible are about women—such as Ruth and Esther—this letter of mine is the only book addressed to a woman, this Elect Lady.

Now, Elect Lady of the twentieth century, I desire to give you the same message, and I am glad that the men who put the Bible together realized this and were led of God to make it available to you, too. You, who are living in the latter days, need this warning perhaps even more than the Lady to whom I first wrote.

As I told that Elect Lady then, I tell you now that I love you very much, as do so many in the Church. I am happy to see that your children are living as they should, following the truth and obeying God's commands. It tells me that you have taught them well.

I do want to remind you of the most important commandment God ever gave us, that Christians should love one another. You have heard this many times already, but sometimes we forget it as we work together. But if we truly love God, we will love one another as He loved us.

Now when it comes to hospitality, you should open your homes to those in need. Paul once reminded us that as we do this, we might even entertain angels unawares. However, I must warn you not to entertain false teachers and leaders who are against the truth and against Christ. They might lead you astray by flattering you with their kind words of appreciation for giving them a place to stay and food to eat. You must remember the truth which you have been taught and don't let yourself be put in a position of having to listen to wrong doctrines just because these people are guests in your home.

If anyone comes to teach you, and does not believe as Jesus taught, or in Jesus for who He truly was, do not invite them into your house. Don't encourage these false teachers in any way, for if you do, you will make yourself a partner with them in wickedness.

Well, I would like to say more, but I won't be able to write it in this letter.

May God strengthen you and bless you as you continue to do His will, my Elect Lady of the twentieth century.

Sincerely,
John

Dear Father in heaven, thank you for your provision of protection in my life as a believer in you. I do appreciate all those good pastors, elders, and teachers who have shared your truth with me. And, most of all, I thank you for your written word to me, that I may continually refer to it for wisdom and guidance. Help me to be faithful in reading and meditating upon it that your Word may be hidden within my heart. Amen.

THE BRIDE OF
THE LAMB OF GOD

THE WOMAN CHOSEN TO BE
THE BRIDE OF CHRIST

Eph. 5:22-27; Rev. 19:5-9; 21:2-5, 9-27

And the Spirit and the bride say, Come. And let him that heareth say, Come. And let him that is athirst come. And whosoever will, let him take the water of life freely.   Rev. 22:17

What words can describe that marriage supper of the Lamb which will take place soon! It will be the time of greatest rejoicing for all of heaven and of earth because Jesus, the spotless Lamb of God, will be united with His holy, beautiful Bride. It will be the climax of all history, for "His-story" will be complete!

Even John, in the revelation of the future which God had given him, could not fully describe the lovely Bride at this wedding celebration except to picture her as the beautiful, holy city Jerusalem coming down from heaven. She was full of glory, made of precious stones and lined with streets of pure gold. She was a city of eternal light with all sorrow and darkness banished forever.

Paul had earlier described the Bride as the glorious Church, holy and without blemish, which Jesus will present to himself. Because He had shed His blood upon the cross, He paid the price required by God for the sacrifice for sin. Each one who accepts this work of atonement by Jesus becomes part of His Church, His Bride. Praise God!

The Bride as the Holy City and the Bride as the Church gives us two insights into this woman God has chosen for the Bride of His own Son. First, as the New Jerusalem, the Holy City, she will come down from God out of heaven (Rev. 21:2). God will make her ready by His grace, His mercy, His love. It's only possible because He sent Jesus into the world as a sacrifice for sin. Then He sent the Holy Spirit to do a work in sanctifying her, a work which is now going on. God is making the Bride perfectly beautiful, adorning her with many jewels and the most precious of metals, clothing of "wrought gold" and "raiment of needlework" (Ps. 45:13, 14). He will present this Bride of Brides to Jesus.

The Bride also has a part in her preparation (Rev. 19:7). She is making herself clean by confessing her sins (1 John 1:9), and by submitting to the cleansing in God's Word (Eph. 5:26). Her garment is going through the purifying fire of trials and tribulation. The wedding gown is being embroidered by the Holy Spirit as the Bride has allowed Him to work in her.

In this book, we have looked at the lives of sixty-four women that God has given us in His Word and have meditated upon the personal applications each one has for us. To bring His Word to a climax, God gives us a picture of the woman *we* are to be, the Bride of His own Son, Jesus Christ! She is the ultimate Woman in the Word!

Along with this most envied of positions, He gives us a work to do as we anticipate that great marriage supper when we at last will see our Bridegroom face to face! Like the other women in the Bible, we have a purpose, a job to do that His will might be accomplished on earth. God has given to the Bride, the Church, besides the gift of the Holy Spirit, the challenge of calling others to Jesus that they too might be part of Him. Together we have the joy of saying:

> Come to Jesus—He is the Savior, the Lamb of God, sent into this world to save each of us from the sin and punishment which befell all mankind in the Garden of Eden.

> Come to Jesus—He has died for your sin. He wants you to have abundant life now as well as eternal life to come.

> Come to Jesus—He is the one who loves you beyond understanding and who waits now to be your Husband forever.

Jesus, the Bridegroom, is ready and waiting. He wants to consummate the marriage. When the work has been completed and His perfect time is come, Jesus will say, "Surely I come quickly" (Rev. 22:20). May each one of us who are part of the Bride be ready to respond with hearts of overflowing love and anticipation, "Even so, come, Lord Jesus!"

Dear Heavenly Father, I cannot comprehend your love toward me. I cannot imagine all that you have done to save me, let alone all that you are now doing to prepare me to be that lovely Bride for your dear Son. Lord, I cannot understand, but I do thank you from the bottom of my heart. I look forward to that marriage supper of the Lamb. Even so, come, Lord Jesus. Amen.